Praise for JUST ASK SPIRIT

"An empowering must-read guide to emotional and spiritual healing! In *Just Ask Spirit*, Sherianna masterfully helps the reader understand the profound relationship between mental health and spirituality. Within the pages, you'll discover her tried-and-true CLEANSE system, along with the exercises, tools, and techniques for building resiliency, overcoming obstacles, and developing your intuition! *Just Ask Spirit* serves as a sacred reminder of what's possible when we unify our emotions and spirituality."

—**Linda Joy,** publisher of *Aspire Magazine* and
Mindset Elevation Coach, www.AspireMag.net

"This book is more than a guide—it is a soul-stirring companion for those ready to step into their fullest emotional and spiritual potential."

—**Bernadette Logue,** spiritual coach and author
of *Your Soul Journey Simplified*

"Sherianna Boyle has once again illuminated the profound power of emotional processing. Using her signature CLEANSE method, she gracefully guides readers into their emotions as a divine resource for connecting with Spirit, offering transformative practices that heal and empower."

—**Carmen Turner-Schott, MSW, LISW,** author of *Your Astrological Energy: Maximize the Power of Your Birth Chart, Sun Signs, Houses & Healing,* and *Moon Signs, Houses & Healing*

T0357737

"*Just Ask Spirit* takes the guesswork out of asking, providing readers with a valuable resource for processing your emotions, as well as asking and receiving guidance from Spirit. This book is both enlightening and practical, offering valuable insights and strategies for achieving greater harmony and self-awareness."

—**George Lizos,** bestselling author of *Protect Your Light, Secrets of Greek Mysticism,* and *Ancient Manifestation Secrets*

"Sherianna Boyle has brought forward a beautiful illustration of soul empowerment and practical avenues to connect deeper to the emotional and spiritual. I wish they taught this in schools. A profound read for anyone looking to connect to their higher self through deeper emotional awareness in an effective way."

—**Jacob Cooper, LCSW,** bestselling author of *Life After Breath* and *The Wisdom of Jacob's Ladder*

"*Just Ask Spirit* is a transformative masterpiece that bridges the realms of emotion and Spirit with profound clarity and depth. This book offers a unique exploration of how our emotions serve as a divine compass, guiding us toward a deeper connection with our Spirit guides."

—**Amy Leigh Mercree,** medical intuitive and bestselling author of *Aura Alchemy: Learn to Sense Energy Fields, Interpret the Color Spectrum, and Manifest Success*

JUST ASK SPIRIT

FREE YOUR EMOTIONS TO ENERGIZE INTUITION AND DISCOVER PURPOSE

SHERIANNA BOYLE

BESTSELLING AUTHOR OF *EMOTIONAL DETOX*

Health Communications, Inc.
Boca Raton, Florida

www.hcibooks.com

Library of Congress Cataloging-in-Publication Data
is available through the Library of Congress

©2025 Sherianna Boyle

ISBN-13: 978-07573-2528-1 (Paperback)
ISBN-10: 07573-2528-9 (Paperback)
ISBN-13: 978-07573-2529-8 (ePub)
ISBN-10: 07573-2529-7 (ePub)

Publisher: Health Communications, Inc.
          301 Crawford Boulevard, Suite 200
          Boca Raton, FL 33432-3762

Cover, interior design, and formatting by Larissa Hise Henoch

Mom, this one is for you.

CONTENTS

PREFACE

In the human world, depending on our perception, we experience emotions either as a gain or loss of energy, which is our level of awareness or consciousness. The challenge is that when we lose energy by denying, ignoring, or reacting to emotions, the memory of who we truly are—a spiritual being in a human body—dissipates. In other words, emotional stress prevents us from knowing and connecting to our soul's purpose. However, when we experience emotions on the *spiritual* or soul level, our energy doesn't fluctuate or drop. In other words, we don't ride the same highs and lows.

Many people believe their purpose is a *thing*, something they must acquire or achieve. In this book you'll come to understand that purpose is about getting to know who you truly are. You are more than your job, career, degrees, roles, personality, gender, titles, and bank account. When we choose to overfocus on the things (people, situations, problems, circumstances) outside us, this decreases the chances of really getting to know ourselves as truth (Spirit).

Think of Spirit guides as reflections and connections to who you truly are. They are nonphysical beings of love and light. Depending on your culture, beliefs, and traditions, these forces of energy can be described as archangels, benevolent beings, goddesses, divine feminine, ancestors, life force, nature Spirits—and more.

Here's the thing: You cannot escape the vital role emotions play in your existence. Connecting with Spirit is the key to your spiritual evolution and purpose. To put it simply, when you choose to shut down your emotions, it is no different than saying to your Spirit guides, "I don't want or need your support." Yet, when you allow yourself to feel, you open to divine love, unconditional support, guidance, healing, and abundance.

While this may seem a bit overwhelming at first, I want you to know the ball is (and always will be) in your court. You have a choice: get to know your emotions, their value, and how they can help you transform emotional stress and connect you to the Spirit realms, or not. It is up to you. Yet if you are drawn to this book, my guess is something inside you knows and this truth can no longer be avoided. Now, it's just a matter of learning how to ask.

For some of you that is easier said than done.

If you ever had a question or request and then suddenly lost the courage to ask, you know what I mean. Maybe you wanted to set a boundary, request time off from work, sensed distress from a co-worker, and told yourself it wasn't the right time. Or perhaps you are a person who used to be really great at asking questions but then received some discouraging or negative feedback, and now you associate asking with conflict or pain. Or maybe you feel like you are always in a rush and just don't have time. Sound familiar? If so, I totally get it. I have been there too. Yet here is something worth pondering: *If you don't ask, how will you ever learn how to fully receive? And if you can't receive, how will you ever truly be happy?*

To ask means a part of you is willing to let something in. It may be knowledge, feedback, guidance, clarity, wisdom, love, support, or connection. As you can imagine, being able to let something in often coincides with the ability to let something go—like fear, doubt, worry, and guilt, which only stall your progress. Inside these pages, you will of course learn the words, gestures, and phrases for asking Spirit, but more importantly you learn the ways in which you can receive. Once you get this, the bridge between asking and receiving is built. This state of oneness, of unity, is often the way we experience Spirit.

Now, I'm pretty sure you have experienced the consequences of not asking—we all have. Perhaps you signed a contract without inquiring about the details or took on extra work without asking for additional pay. When these life lessons happen, and they will, you can lose your stamina, courage, self-confidence, energy, and more. This can lead to life feeling like a to-do list or a relentless cycle of fulfilling the constant demands made on you. It can happen to the best of us when asking and receiving are experienced as two separate actions.

I bet you are looking forward to doing things differently.

What I have learned is that we often perceive asking as a sign of distress, failure, weakness, neediness, or overwhelm. The challenge is that these types of responses cause us to suppress our emotions rather than process them. When they are allowed to stagnate in this way it harms not only our psychological well-being but our physical too.

I'm sure you are wondering by now how this level of asking can be possible. How do you transform the barrage of life's demands into developing resilience, strength, peace, and harmony? All I can say is, as asking and receiving become one, so do emotions and your Spirit.

How this book may differ from other spiritual books you have read is it includes a mindful system I created called *Cleanse*. Using this system, I guide you into the world of Spirit through the processing of your emotions. When you practice this, you will feel calm, grounded, and relaxed. From this state, I teach you not only how to fully receive Spirit but also how your emotions play an integral role in *being* Spirit.

As you get to know Spirit in this way, your relationship with it, yourself, and others will grow in profound ways. Soon you'll see how Spirit doesn't just show you healing, it *activates* healing. It doesn't just give you clarity, it *activates* clarity—you get the point. And when you begin to ask in this way, you notice the harsh demands or unrealistic expectations—internal and external, conscious and unconscious—will begin to dissolve.

Right now, you may be wondering what I mean by Spirit, and I assure you, we will get into that in Chapter 1. For now, know this book is not about getting you to believe something you don't or to act, think, or feel anything that isn't authentic to you. Spirit is not a religion. While religion can supply a foundation or road map for spirituality, as well as morals and values, that is not what this book is about. If anything, it is about inviting you to put more faith in yourself.

The truth of the matter is you *are* already Spirit. Just as you can live your entire life with an inner gift such as drawing or singing and never really develop it, the same is true for Spirit. It is already within. Should you choose to nourish your connection to Spirit through Cleanse and try the exercises I have provided in this book, you'll have all it takes to understand the true meaning of asking and receiving.

Welcome to *Just Ask Spirit!*

INTRODUCTION

Emotions evoke the memory of Spirit.

As I wrote this book, I conducted over a hundred interviews with my Emotional Detox coaching clients and via my *Just Ask Spirit* podcast. I talked to all sorts of people from psychic mediums, animal communicators, shamans, neuroanatomists, energy healers, herbalists, physicians, nutritionists, poets, lawyers, transformational coaches, psychologists, and more. Basically, if someone had "seen the light," had a near-death experience (NDE), heard a voice, channeled a saint or loved one, altered their life through a spiritual event, experienced divine inspiration or a breakthrough understanding about esoteric wisdom, mental health, intuition, or theology—I wanted to hear their story. More importantly, I wanted to *understand* how it shaped the way they defined and connected to Spirit.

In these many conversations, Spirit was described as *consciousness, the energy of inspiration, love, nature, life-force energy, essence,*

Source, and more. I learned so much, but what was interesting to me was no one really homed in on the connection between *emotions* and Spirit. That is one of the many reasons I decided to write this book.

Here is the thing I've learned: when you allow yourself to fully process meaning, you allow the energy (vibration) of your emotions to move inside you. Your mind gets quiet, and as this occurs, old habits of resisting the moment dissipate as your connection to your higher self and Spirit begins to emerge . . . *if you let it.*

As you embark on this journey, it's likely the similarities between Spirit and emotions will become so familiar you will have a tough time separating the two, nor would you want to. Similar to the way a good book goes along with a warm cup of tea, you'll find the two (emotions and Spirit) complement each other quite well. Spending time with yourself in this way will likely lead to newfound realizations, aha! moments, or a deep and knowing sigh or two. These internal shifts are not only normal; they're necessary.

Right now, you might have one foot in emotional reactivity and another dabbling in spirit. If my higher self could speak to your higher self right now, it would say, "Choose one." With that said, I know I have a bit of an advantage here as I already have a sense of where we are heading. Yet I promise there's a path where you'll come to see that emotions and Spirit are one and the same. This is the one I encourage you to take, and this book explains how.

With learning comes unlearning most of the things you were taught about emotions. You know, how some are bad and some are good, some are weak while others are strong? As you embark on this journey of asking Spirit, there will be times you'll recognize the ways the conditioning placed on emotions has influenced your beliefs in both positive and negative ways. Some of those limiting beliefs may still be hanging around, but have faith—they can and will dissolve through this process! The same goes for some of the things you may have been taught around Spirit. I want you to know this book is not about judging the past, reopening your wounds, or pointing a finger at your upbringing; it's about having the courage to ask for, and more importantly, to receive all that is available to you.

As I wrote this book, I learned quite a bit; one thing is how exploring emotions can only take you so far, and the second thing is exploring Spirit without guidance along the way can *also* limit your potential. The bottom line is when it comes to asking Spirit, you need both. Because at the core, we are all Spirit, *and* we all have emotions. This gives us the ability to connect to infinite resources beyond the things we rely on now, much in the way our computers connect to the Internet.

Yet this can't happen, at least not to its fullest extent, when emotions are ignored or minimized. Here's the thing: it takes more energy (effort) to control (hold back) an emotion than it does to allow it to move through you. The good news is with practice (and yes, it is a practice) the barriers of inner resistance will fade, only to be replaced by the translucent energy of Spirit.

As a result, you'll find yourself fully equipped, ready, open, and willing to receive. You may not have had opportunities to receive before. Perhaps someone expressed their love or kindness toward you, but you were not in a place to accept it. In a case like that, you likely had old wounds getting in the way. I assure you the method of asking Spirit that I teach here can help.

To do this, we'll dive into the parallels between Spirit and emotions, and as this occurs, you'll begin to see the correlation between blocked emotions and restricting Spirit, and consequently how a constrained Spirit can block emotional processing. Through the exploration of bodily sensations and energy practices, I'll help you discover how emotions can build the bridge not just to your own Spirit but to your divine team of spiritual guides.

With that said, don't expect this process to be perfect. It's common to slide back into reactivity through worrisome thoughts or restrictive thinking now and then. See these as opportunities to acquire a keener sense of awareness. Should you have an off day here and there, remember:

When you value your emotions, you honor Spirit.

And when you honor Spirit, you value your emotions.

Either way, you can't go wrong. Here's the thing: if you follow but one rule throughout your journey:

Feel first, then ask.

✿

From time to time in this book, I will share messages, insights, and feedback I've received from Spirit. I want you to know that, like you, I am Spirit, and therefore, we are always growing, learning, and being guided. When describing myself, I often say I'm an author, teacher, mom, founder of Emotional Detox coaching, wife, energy healer, yoga instructor, and businessperson. That is how I spend my time. Lots of people come to me because they've heard I'm pretty good at listening to and translating the energy and wisdom of Spirit, but I don't consider myself to be a psychic or medium. I get more joy from guiding others as they develop these skills for themselves.

Just Ask Spirit is my eleventh book. You might wonder, *Wow! How does she write all those books?* Honestly, eleven books is just me benefiting from knowing how to connect to my higher self. Once you have this ability, you truly open a doorway to a universe of possibilities.

SO HOW DOES IT WORK?

I've divided *Just Ask Spirit* into three parts. I recommend you start this book from the beginning and progress chapter by chapter until you get to Part 3: Choose: The 7777 Pathway. Everything in Part 1 and 2 prepares you for what happens in Part 3.

Part 1 begins with information about Spirit, emotions, how they can help amplify your connection while helping you become spiritually strong and heathy. At the end of the chapters in Part 1, you'll find *Cleanse Highlights*. C-L-E-A-N-S-E is my acronym for a seven-step mindful approach for processing your emotions. Because each step is mindful and mediative in nature, once you get going, they feel less like steps and more like a centering, calming practice. Cleanse is the structure, the foundation, I use for both emotional processing and connecting to Spirit. In Part 1, I provide you with a sense of what Cleanse looks and feels like by providing you with information about each step at the bottom of each chapter.

As you enter Part 2, you will begin to see how the Cleanse evolves into a practice for both emotional processing and asking Spirit. Part 2 includes spiritual tools for channeling (gathering information) from Spirit through your senses. It is then you will get to know the modalities such as automatic writing, mantras, mediation, breathwork, automatic coloring, Spirit dance, and Spirit walks for channeling Spirit. At the end of each chapter in Part 2, you'll find *Spirit Messages*, which are channeled insights I received either through my work with clients or during my personal practice over the years. Think of them as self-care tips, some of which can be quite life-changing.

Please note that occasionally I'll guide you through some breathing exercises. Since breathwork comes with some contraindications, if you have a history of seizures, stroke, respiratory problems such as asthma, pregnancy, or high or low blood pressure, please consult with your doctor before taking part.

Part 3 is all about what I call the *7777 Pathway*. There are seven steps to processing your emotions, seven steps to asking Spirit, and two seven-step practices—the Element and the Archangel. The Element deepens your spiritual connection by teaching you how to process your emotions and connect to Spirit by tuning into the consciousness of the elements: air, water, earth, and fire. The Archangel is another powerful method for emotional processing and tuning into the abundance of support, resources, and healing from the celestial realms.

Each of the 7777 Pathways represents the same sentiment: feel *first* and then *ask*. Right now, you may not be quite sure what this means, so I'd like to take a moment to present it this way . . .

- If you were to ask Spirit a question right now, what would you want to know? If the answer to that question doesn't come easily, then that's a fairly good indication you could benefit from Cleansing (i.e., feeling first).

- If on the other hand you know your question, ask yourself if you've asked this question many times before. In other words, are you revisiting the same inquiries that reflect similar emotions (perhaps doubt or insecurity)? What I'm getting at here, is that by moving through the pages and Cleanses in this book, you are really going to get to know the difference between asking as a way to manage the fear and insecurity and asking because you're ready to receive the infinite divine guidance, clarity, and support available from Spirit.

- In other words, you have to wonder, is your "ask" *really* your way of verbalizing or externalizing a worry? If so, you're not alone—I did it too, more times than I care to admit.

- To put your mind at ease about this feeling thing, I invite you to begin by moving through a basic Cleanse. While the ones I share in Part 3 are a different variation, this ought to give you a good idea of the way it will work. Once you get the hang of it, I promise the process will feel quite natural.

CLEANSE

Clear Reactivity: Here is where you will work on mindful practices such as visualizing and connecting to light to help you move out of reactivity and into states of calm and ease. You may also ground and center in other ways such as through gentle neck stretches. This can be done by sitting up tall and tilting your head toward your ear. For example, your right ear might tilt toward your right shoulder. Hold for three seconds. Then return your head to the center and do the other side. Bring your head back to center and notice any release of tension.

Look Inward. Here you repeat what I call a *stem sentence*—a question specific to the Cleanse—out loud.

Your response will be one complete breath: *inhale . . . exhale. . . .* In other words, use breath, not words, to answer the question.

Try it! Repeat this stem sentence out loud: *How I feel in my body right now is . . .* Now breathe: *inhale . . . exhale. . . .*

Emit. Here is where you will recite a mantra. Mantras are words, syllables, or phrases. When repeated, they help free your mind.

While there are dozens of mantras, you will use simple ones called seed sound mantras such as *hum, lam,* or *ram,* which restores balance, harmony, and peace.

Try it! *Inhale . . .* and as you *exhale . . .* allow the sound of *hum* to reverberate through you.

Activate. Here you notice and observe energy. This gives you information about how to know when you are connected to your own Spirit as with your Spirit guides. With practice you will sense things like changes in temperature, tingly sensations, calm, visualizations (such as light), sometimes words, or even images.

During the Cleanses, I'll encourage you to lean into any colors, scents, or tingly sensations you are picking up on by giving yourself permission to relax even further. This allows you to clear and transmute old stuck energy, beliefs, or emotions into higher vibrations of calm, love, and joy.

Nourish. Now you'll practice learning how, by being an observer (witnessing energy), you are teaching yourself to allow and receive all the divine support available to you. This is all explained in Part 2, where I teach you how to channel.

Surrender. It's time to speak "I allow" statements out loud. "I allow" is your free will statement. These may include *I allow grounding, I allow confidence, I allow guidance, I allow clarity, I allow reassurance.*

With Spirit, your free will matters (more on this later). You have the right to choose to connect, ask, and receive.

Ease. Here is where you *become* Spirit—there really is no separation. As you embody this oneness, you'll repeat "I am" statements out loud. For example, *I am clarity, I am wisdom, I am reassurance, I am energy, I am Spirit.*

Now that you have a better sense of the way Cleanse works, you can better appreciate how each step supports the next, moving the process forward as an effortless flow of energy. When you do a Cleanse and combine it with the spiritual exercises provided in Part

3, you'll find yourself with a solid practice for both asking and receiving guidance, healing, clarity, and wisdom from Spirit.

Since these practices also help you process your emotions, don't be surprised if you start to notice improvement in other areas of your life such as your overall self-esteem, confidence, communication skills, intuition, emotional regulation, and trust.

After moving through the entire book one time, feel free to focus exclusively on Part 3 as you continue a daily or weekly practice.

Now, take a nice deep breath, relax your body, soften your eyes, and let's begin!

PART 1

INVITE: EMOTIONS, PURPOSE, AND EVOKING SPIRIT

*Turn to your emotions as
a resource for evoking Spirit, and they
will bring you closer to your light.*

CHAPTER 1

WHAT IS SPIRIT?

I became curious about Spirit when I was thirteen years old, walking by a church on my way to my summer babysitting job. The doors were open, and the music of the choir drew me closer. I entered and sat in the last pew, listening to the beautiful hymns. When the choir stopped, I left. I did this many times throughout the summer. I never stayed long enough for anyone to get to know me or ask my name. It didn't occur to me that I might be rude or disruptive. The smile on people's faces when they saw me sitting by myself was enough to let me know they didn't mind. Years later my parents told me it was a Baptist church, and although I was raised Catholic, they never once mentioned it. They said they didn't want to dissuade me from attending, and I'm so glad they didn't because what happened there was that *I started to feel*. You see, before this, our family had been through years of trauma. In many ways, I felt I was born into a crisis, and at the age of thirteen years, perhaps for the first time ever, I was allowing myself a moment to breathe, which makes sense since the Latin word for spirit is *spiritus*, translated as "breath, breathing, soul, courage, or vigor." It was around this same age that I started to speak and receive messages from Spirit on my walks alone in nature and through the pages of my journal. These are some of my earliest memories of channeling Spirit.

The Course in Miracles says, "The Holy Spirit needs your voice, so it can speak through you: your mind to hold its Messages, so that you can extend Them, where the Holy Spirit directs: and your feet, so that you can go where the Holy Spirit directs, for you to be delivered at last from all perceptions of misery" (*Practicing a Course in Miracles,* p. 353). When Spirit is present, all irrelevant information dissipates so you can pay attention to the heart of the matter as a way to support your soul's journey.

Spending my days with Spirit in this way made me feel whole, nourished, and complete. Yet, as I got older and became more goal focused rather than Spirit focused, I spent less and less time tuning into the energy, vibration of Spirit, until the nudges, insights, and love I once felt faded away. At the time, I hadn't seen how being disconnected from Spirit would have a numbing effect on my emotions. As I grew older, I found myself feeling just enough to get by but not enough to actually heal and discover my purpose. It would be through the devasting circumstances of my marriage, where I would need to make a choice between numbing and feeling. I chose to feel, and the voice of Spirit returned with the guidance, clarity, love, and support I needed to rebuild my marriage into a partnership where tremendous love, respect, and trust could exist.

The Bible refers to Spirit as a vehicle for a new direction, through scriptures such as:

"But after they had come up out of the water again, the Spirit of the Lord carried Philip away" (Acts 8:39). "Now the Lord is the Spirit, and where the Spirit of the Lord is, there is freedom" (2 Corinthians 3:17).

The New Testament also refers to our ability to communicate with Spirit. Romans 8:9 tells us, "It is this human spiritual nature that enables continuing conversation with the divine Spirit: You, however, are not in the realm of the flesh but are in the realm of the Spirit, if indeed the Spirit of God lives in you."

The verse I feel most connected to and curious about is from Mark 11:24: "Jesus said, ask and you shall receive." What I have learned is feeling is just another way of receiving.

No matter whether you are religious or not, Spirit is the part of us that is infinite. It is the energy of bravery, hope, unconditional love, reassurance, direction, healing, and more. Spirit (like what happens when emotions are in a processing state) is what moves you from the inside out. Spirit can be a gentle nudge to look in a certain direction, a sudden yet subtle break from ruminating thoughts, a sense that a change is coming, the feeling you get when someone pours you a cup of coffee, or a whisper of hope along the horizon. Spirit can be a moment of stillness just before everyone in the house wakes, a sensation of calm when you gaze at the ocean, or when a noisy room suddenly falls silent. Spirit can also be a surge of determination during the last pushes of hard labor when a baby is born, the voice that tells you to call your sister for no reason only to discover she's received sad news, or the courage to get yourself out of bed, wash your face, and begin again. Spirit is holiness, purity, light, wisdom, and essence all in one. When your emotions are in flow, thoughts dissipate, yet Spirit remains.

WHAT ARE SPIRITS?

From the time I was twelve years old until I was eighteen, my family lived in a Victorian home just over the Massachusetts' border in New York State. Built in the early 1800s, our house was coated with three shades of pink paint. I have vivid memories of my parents drinking coffee next to the large windows in the kitchen. They talked about work, finances, house projects, all the things parents discuss. But then the conversations stopped. When I was in high school my parents separated, and their divorce was finalized around my eighteenth birthday.

My mother did a beautiful job filling our home with antiques and decor from the Victorian era, yet it contained something else as well: *energy*. We often heard noises, knocks, clangs, and voices when we were sleeping or sitting quietly. Once, Mom reported waking up in the middle of the night feeling like something had touched her.

For me, this led to fear and confusion. On the one hand, when I went outside (often with my journal and a pen), connecting with my Spirit felt peaceful, calm, loving, and supported. Yet inside our house I felt guarded and uneasy. Between the growing tension between my parents and the strange energy inside the house, I found myself becoming adept at turning my emotions off and on as a way to protect myself. After all, feeling more was the last thing I needed, right? *Not so.*

Later I learned that the word *spirits* (plural) can refer to the energy of people who have passed away or returned to function as a guide. Spirits are what I was picking up on in that old house, the energy of a dead person or people—what some may call a ghost.

Regardless of what it was, I knew it freaked me out. At the time, I had no idea I could ask for and acquire protection from spirits.

Looking back, I'm not sure what frightened me more: the energy I was picking up on, or the stories I would tell myself when I heard or felt that energy. Mom didn't seem to mind it. Instead, she was quite intrigued and dealt with our "ghosts" by going to the library and local antique shops to see if she could dig up the archives of those who had previously lived in the house.

Hold your breath enough times, and it's likely your muscles will tense up. As tension increases so does fear, and before you know it, shallow breathing becomes a way of life until you develop symptoms such as irritability, exhaustion, restlessness, and even pain. Because my nervous system was already dysregulated from years of trauma, I became someone who was easily startled. As this tension increased, most of my attention became focused on bettering myself so I could get away and start my life.

Can you relate? Maybe you lived or worked with someone who was unpredictable, critical, poked fun at you, or was depressed. Without realizing it, you may have found yourself tiptoeing around or avoiding this person altogether—figuratively and literally holding your breath—to manage the tension. Each time we restrict our breath we impede Spirit, and as you'll see later in this book, we need to correct this imbalance if we want to develop spiritually.

Spirit (singular) is the nonphysical part of you described in the *Oxford English Dictionary* as "the seat of emotions, soul or character." When your emotions are in flow, you are responding as Spirit. This gives you stamina, trust in the process, and belief in what is possible (even if you can't yet see it) to manifest whatever you are looking to create—whether it be a new job or a sense of purpose or direction.

One of the ways you know your emotions are in flow (or that you are with Spirit) is when your perception changes for the better. For example, you might take things less personally or be more accountable for your thoughts and actions. These kinds of transformations allow you to expand your level of consciousness, which means you are better able to trust your gut and follow what feels right.

While spirits are often referred to as the energy of those who have passed, *Spirit* is the energy of consciousness connected to Source (God, the Divine, the Creator, the One, for me I tend to refer to it as the Christ consciousness, Holy Spirit, or God). Through the development of consciousness, we can activate godlike qualities within ourselves, especially our ability to love.

LEVELS OF CONSCIOUSNESS

I once had a client named Sara who was very intuitive. Sara told me about a time when she stayed at a hotel in New York City, not knowing it had a reputation for being haunted. As she slept, she felt an energy pulling on her feet. She was so terrified that she made her husband get up in the middle of the night and change their room. These kinds of odd and creepy incidents continued to happen to her over several years. When she was alone in her office, the paper shredder would spontaneously turn on and start shredding. Sure, it could have been a fluke, but for Sara it felt like the hotel incident. She contacted me, initially looking for emotional support, but when she realized I channeled Spirit, she decided to ask for guidance on how to deal with these energies.

Whenever I work with a client, I make a point to first guide them through a Cleanse, which in this case is what I did with Sara. This gives each one of us an opportunity to become more aware and conscious. From my work as an Emotional Detox coach, I recognize how emotional reactivity can come from the subconscious (unresolved fears, ego), while Spirit comes from the conscious (truth). Without emotions in flow, we run the risk of bumping into the part of our ego that tries to control, fix, fight with, or figure out what is happening. This is not Spirit. Here is what our Cleanse looked like:

CLEANSE

Clear Reactivity: I guided Sara through a few simple neck stretches and eye movements to help her tone her vagus nerve (more on the vagus nerve in the Cleanse highlight at the end of this chapter). After these brief exercises I provided Sara with a mudra (hand gesture) for calm, safety, and protection. Then we moved to the next step.

Look Inward: I provided Sara with some stem sentences to repeat out loud and then follow with her breath: *inhale ... exhale.* ... Worth repeating here is that in this step, you *do not* answer the question; your inhale and exhale *are* your answer. For now, one of Sara's stem sentences included: *Having that experience made me feel* ... inhale ... exhale. ... *Now that I am choosing to connect to the Holy Spirit in me, it makes me feel* ... inhale ... exhale ...

Emit: After inhaling and exhaling a few times, Sara took some deep breaths (inflating her lower abdomen) and exhaled the mantra (sound) *hum* out loud. Her *hum* served two purposes: it allowed Sara to release and transform all the reactivity around those incidents, and it increased energy in her body and energetic field, helping her to connect to her spiritual team for support.

Your spiritual team is made up of anyone or anything you ask to give you support, guidance, or healing. With my client,

I immediately felt the presence of an ascended master. Since I am familiar with the masters through my training as a quantum healer, I knew this being of light was showing up to assist with transforming all negative energy from this incident into pure love and light.

Activate: Now with energy flowing and a sense of inner calm, Sara was able to notice what was happening in the moment. She described tingly sensations around her ankles, which helped her feel more grounded.

Nourish: I encouraged Sara to sit with these sensations a bit longer, allowing them to nourish her fully as her emotions increased in movement, and her connection to her true Spirit provided her with comfort, safety, and love.

Surrender: I guided Sara to repeat her allow statements aloud: *I allow calm, I allow safe, I allow protected, I allow love, and I allow free.* By doing so, Sara was learning how to invite and embody the divine power of Spirit.

Ease: I guided Sara to speak some "I am" statements (remember, the Holy Spirit needs us to speak to direct the energy), which included: *I am safe, I am calm, I am love, and I am free.* This provided her with a sense of oneness and peace.

Sara's story is a wonderful illustration of the power of emotions and Spirit when they are treated as one. You can see (and more importantly feel) how, in her Cleanse, Sara went from remembering an event as terrifying with vibrations of fear to transforming the same situation into calm and peace. It's important to note that the purpose of Cleanse is not to get rid of your emotions; it's about moving them. David R. Hawkins, MD, PhD, described how he brought this to light in his book *Power vs. Force.* He discovered a way to measure emotions through sound, light, and electromagnetic waves coming off the *morphogenetic field* of the human heart. Think of the morphogenetic field as similar to a blueprint of instructions guiding the cell on where to go and what to become. Through his lab work and analysis of peaceful leaders such as Gandhi and Martin Luther King Jr., he determined that when you move beyond defensiveness (which I refer to as reactivity), you embody a higher level of consciousness, and that this embodiment can have profound positive effects on ourselves and the world.

Using the data he collected, he created the Map of Consciousness. Hawkins maps out levels of consciousness, providing insight into what happens as our vibrational frequency increases, like when we breathe or chant mantras. It turns out that as energy (vibration) goes up, ego (which is fear and illusion) dissolves. As this occurs, what separates us from Spirit (ego, fear) *also* dissolves. He found that the emotion of guilt had a vibrational frequency of 60, fear had a frequency of 150, while states of love and peace ranged from 500 and upward.

This all made sense to me because each week for the past couple of years, I've been guiding students through group Cleanses. I open by asking participants, "Is there anything anyone wants to cleanse?" At first, I would hear things like anger, fear, or frustration. Yet as time went on, and as we cleansed, the number of requests decreased. Instead, participants would say things like "You just lead the way." Like being a passenger in a car, the students became less concerned about what we were cleansing and more interested in the experience of cleansing.

In my opinion, what was really happening was that the students and I were discovering that it didn't matter what emotion was cleansed—joy, sorrow, love, fear—because they *all* contain the capacity to move us into higher consciousness when they are permitted to be experienced (i.e., processed) mindfully through consciousness. This is exactly what it feels like when you are connected to Spirit: natural.

Levels of consciousness are states of feeling. Where there is feeling there is space: space for connection, wisdom, spontaneous insights, and more. Yet here is something especially important I want you to know. Right now, you are in Part 1, learning about the Cleanse. This prepares you for the exercises in Part 2 where you'll deepen your connection with Spirit. Note that the exercises you'll experience will guide you into a meditative state, which can often feel like the energy of oneness. This state is ideal for asking Spirit.

If thoughts, stories, or narratives about what is happening in your life clutter your mind, there will be less silent listening or silent receiving. I find silence to be an interesting experience as you usually don't notice silence until after the fact. My spiritual teacher Zoe Marae taught me to pay attention to what happens next. If you don't know what happens next, then there is a chance you didn't move much energy. In other words, if you skip noticing how the energy (inner movement) changes (for example, sensations or tingly increases), it is likely you reverted to thinking. This is where Cleansing can be helpful.

After Cleansing with Sara, there was a natural moment of silence. Soon after, I picked up my pen and paper and started asking specific questions and jotted down some messages.

DIMENSIONS

Wow! Did Spirit have a lot to say! Because I was familiar with Dr. Hawkins's work, I was able to translate the information for Sara. Since the message included something about dimensions, I'll give you a little bit more information on that.

Right now, you may be accustomed to navigating your environment through your five senses: hearing, vision, smell, touch, and taste. Yet through techniques such as meditation, hypnosis, chanting, and energy healing, we know that our senses are not limited to those five. You also have senses that pick up on the movement of energy. For example, you may be able to notice when your body (energy) feels heavy, tight, fluid, constricted, under pressure, open (unrestricted), and light.

Right now, you may be accustomed to thinking about dimensions from a mathematical point of view as measurements of width, height, and depth. Yet this is not the kind of dimension I am referring to when it comes to Spirit. Dimensions in the Spirit world speak to a universal point of view beyond space and time.

While dimensions from the physical are based on finite experiences (a beginning and end), dimensions from a spiritual viewpoint speak to the infinite, where you may experience oneness. As your levels of consciousness increase via emotional processing, your tendency to measure, compare, contrast, attach, control your experiences (that is, energy in motion) decreases. In other words, if you feel tightness in your body, rather than try to fix it (which is a response from a lower dimension), you might turn to your higher consciousness (explained in the next section) as a means for connecting with higher dimensions.

This is one of the many teachings of the spiritual laws of the universe. We learn through these spiritual laws how to let go, trust, and observe our experiences with energy/emotions. As your energy moves, you inevitably become open (increasing intuition) to receiving messages and activations from Spirit.

Here is what Spirit told me about Sara: The reason Sara got so freaked out about the energy is because she experienced it on the physical plane, that is, the dimension where we distinguish light from dark, good from bad. To create a new experience, she had to learn how to view and experience things from a different level or dimension. "*View it from your higher self*," said Spirit.

I shared this message with Sara and then went on to tell her that when she picked up energy, she tried to "deal with it" from the same dimension. However, imagine going up several floors on an elevator and looking out a window. Your view has changed. This also happens as you move consciously into higher dimensions. This is where your higher self and unconditional love exist. Dimensions are not a place but a *state*.

At the time of Sara's frightening experiences, she was simply reflecting her experience as if her elevator was stuck on one floor. When we experience fear, we mirror fear, which means we reflect our inner experience. When we experience panic, we reflect panic. If we go deep inside ourselves, we discover those emotions of fear and panic that already existed within before the triggering event happened. Once we process fear and panic fully, we can move the energy and naturally connect to higher dimensions, viewing things from a different metaphorical floor. This doesn't mean we leave our physical bodies; we simply go inward and start connecting to Spirit and receive inner guidance.

In Sara's case she chose to move physical rooms in the hotel, and as I told Sara, I would place that response more in the action category than reaction. A reaction might have been if she stayed in the same room all night, wide-awake, freaking out wondering what to do. Yet instead, she followed her gut and took action. Then I asked Sara what happened next. Since Sara's responses were more physical (for example, they went home) than spiritual (feeling, for example, calmer), I knew Sara could benefit from a few more of the Chakra Energy Cleanses I provide in Part 3.

Here's the thing: Asking Spirit is like getting a play-by-play of a football game. Just when you think you know where things are going, in a matter of seconds it changes. One thing I love about working with Spirit is that you learn how to be patient and flexible. This is because unlike the mind (brain) where thoughts can sometimes feel stuck or rigid, Spirit can't really be captured in words or even actions because you are working with limitless, infinite energy.

For example, after guiding Sara through a Cleanse, our question for Spirit shifted from "How do I deal with these unsettling energies?" to "Is there something I need to clear so I can be able to respond from my higher self?" When it comes time to ask Spirit questions, I encourage you to always feel first and then ask because as your vibration increases, your sense of clarity improves. If you are thinking that asking and feeling are two separate practices, you can breathe a sigh of relief as I have put it all together as one practice. Soon you will recognize that feeling, knowing, trusting, or guiding is your *next*. Although my teacher never framed it this way, now I fully understand what it meant when Jesus said in Mark 11:24, "Ask and you shall receive."

The receiving *is* the next!

HIGHER SELF

Higher self is something I've heard described as "a state of being in the absence of ego." When I asked Spirit to give me more information on what it means to be in your higher self, I heard these words: *universal intelligence . . . collective consciousness.* The higher self has no judgment and is very protective. When you are connected to your higher self, you are no longer functioning as separate *from.* Instead, you are experiencing yourselves as a *part of* something greater. Higher self, there is no hierarchy, no separation; everything just *is.* You no longer need to fight, control, manage, or hide from lower energies, or emotions, for that matter. Higher self is when you and your Spirit are fully connected. You are operating from a different level, a level where peace, forgiveness, compassion, and patience often live. Therefore, when you find yourself feeling like you want to be gentler, kinder to yourself and others, it's likely you are connected to your higher self.

I encourage you to treat your higher self like a spirit (which it is). In other words, you can ask your higher self questions. Simply say, *I call upon my higher self to learn more about . . .* Or, *I call upon my higher self to receive guidance about . . .*

Some ways to strengthen your higher self/Spirit connection are to keep a gratitude journal, recite affirmations, create a prayer altar, meditate, or my favorite: praise. Praise God, praise love, praise life, praise breath, uplift the energy by singing your praises. It's like what I saw in that Baptist church as a kid. Although I did not stand up and clap along, I felt their glory, and as this occurred, I found myself in "the next," experiencing the vibrations of receiving.

Today I don't really attend physical church. Instead, the altar is in my heart, it is me connected to my higher self, engaging in activities such as walking in nature, writing to be with Spirit, teaching yoga, anything that helps me to soften the voice of the ego and negative thinking. When you are in a state of praise or appreciation, you're choosing to transcend the pain or past traumas your soul has endured and move into higher states of consciousness (opening to higher dimensions) where true healing and transformation occurs.

Author and spiritual teacher Eckhart Tolle also speaks to this subject, writing: "There are two dimensions to who you are. The first is what I sometimes call the 'surface I'—the person with a past and a future. The second dimension to who you are is what I like to call the 'Deep I.'" He describes the gap between thoughts (via silence in meditation) as a way to access the "Deep I." The Deep I (as I interpret it) is the part of you that *just knows*. You can't explain it, but you are drawn in a certain direction or toward a certain feeling.

Another view of dimensions comes from author and hypnotherapist Dolores Cannon, a pioneer of past-life regression. She teaches that there are an infinite number of dimensions and that we can access these dimensions through practices such as hypnotherapy and meditation. Through these kinds of practices, we can take our soul's journey, tapping into lives we have lived before. Understanding our past lives gives us insight into our current journey, according to Cannon.

While the science around the notion that there are parallel universes is still sparse, this ancient understanding is undergoing a resurgence in modern popularity. I learned about dimensions through studying quantum physics and quantum healing. Quantum physics looks at the nature of energy at a subatomic level; in quantum healing you learn how to access these levels to get to the root of patterns of energy. For example, if someone has physical pain, in quantum healing we want to know more about the pattern of energy that may be contributing to the pain.

A pattern can be made up of beliefs, thoughts, memories, and blocked emotions. Through spiritual practices such as meditation we're taught to use our psychic centers (our "third eye" or our heart) to remotely view our clients. For example, our client might physically be on the table in front of us. We learned how to close our eyes and tune into our psychic abilities as a means for sensing, feeling, moving, and unblocking energy. The example that follows gives you a little bit more insight into how this works.

Julie came to me newly retired from her thirty years of service in a school district. She was interested in my work because she wanted to learn more about emotional processing as a way to open up new doorways for the next chapter of her life. I took Julie through a basic version of the Cleanse just to give her a sense of how the system worked. New to the process, Julie reported at the end of the seven steps that she felt calmer and more connected to her body. I then asked Spirit how to proceed to the next Cleanse. In other words, I wanted Spirit to guide me on what to focus on next. Suddenly, I was drawn to these words, "connected to my body." As you learn to ask Spirit, you'll notice messages like this too. One of the ways you're connected to Spirit is you become laser focused. So rather than try to "fix" or "figure out" others, you lean into what you sense, and hear.

I listened to Spirit, and together we Cleansed around this idea of being connected to her body. After the second Cleanse, Julie reported some clarity. She said, "I realized I've spent most of my life *not* connected to my body." I reframed her statement and asked her if what she meant was that she had spent most of her life detached from her body.

"Yes, that is exactly what I do, I detach so I can't feel anything."

Spirit always gets us to truth.

Then I asked her, "How do you know when you are detached from your body?" (This is where I get her involved in the process.) She replied, "I get lost in my thoughts and stop paying attention to what is happening around me." In other words, she loses her "next" (ask and you shall receive). Spirit delivered, and Julie received the message. She then was able to translate that message to me; by doing so, she is becoming a messenger of God. *A Course of Miracles* states, "As God's messenger you fulfill your role by accepting God's messages for yourself, and then demonstrating that you have understood Them, by giving Them away (*Practicing a Course of Miracles*, p. 352).

Here is something interesting. I once received an energy healing session from another healer, and afterward she told me that she had asked Spirit to numb my emotions of pain. I remember thinking, *What? Why would you ever do that? My emotions are so valuable.* What I know now is that the healer believed that was what I needed. Yet to me, that felt like a reaction on the healer's part, something they could have benefited from Cleansing before doing energy healing work on me.

As healers, light workers, or students of energy, it is very important for us to do our own inner work. This means to regularly clean your energy. Like the way you might clear the clutter in your home, you want to clear the fears, judgments, as well as old stuck emotions from your body. Keep in mind your body includes energy centers called chakras. This is partially why I designed the Cleanses around clearing your chakras in Part 3. As author Caroline Myss states in her book *Anatomy of the Spirit*, "Each of these energy centers contains a universal spiritual life-lesson that we must learn as we evolve into higher consciousness (p. 68). Through the Cleanse you can work with the energy of the chakras to unravel the lesson, take in the learnings, evolve, and align with your true purpose.

Reflection

- Take a moment to reflect on what Spirit means to you. How do you know when Spirit is present in your life? There are no right or wrong answers. Write down some thoughts in this book, a notebook, or a journal.
- How do you know when your energy (emotions) is cluttered? How does that show up in your mind or body?
- Now ponder this: What practices or activities do you currently have in your life to help you connect with Spirit? What keeps your energy in flow? There are no right or wrong answers here; it is all about recognizing how you can consciously choose to show up to yourself.

SHOWING UP

Here's the way I see it: You have two choices. You can live your life as a human being who believes and connects to something greater or live your life as a spiritual being in a human body who *is* something greater. In my experience when I believe in something greater, there is still a part of me that feels "less than." Perhaps this is due to my years of attending Catholic school. Although I liked the smaller environment, I would constantly tell my mother, "They're trying to brainwash me."

"How so?" she would ask.

"By making me go to confession, they want me to believe I am a sinner," I replied.

Now, I have no idea what they did or did not say to me back then, but what I do remember is the way it made me feel: ashamed. Did they cause the shame? Probably not. It's likely I showed up to school with it already inside me.

Yet when I remind myself of the scripture passage, "Ask and you shall receive," because I know what it feels like to process an emotion and the way that allows me to notice what is next (calm, peace), I have come to understand the presence of Christ, God, Creator, Source as the energy (consciousness) produced within me of Spirit. Then I can transition from connecting to something greater to having something greater within me.

I'm not saying the feeling of showing up happens overnight, but that doesn't mean it won't happen. What I'm saying is when you recite the "I am" statements in the Cleanse, know you *are* that.

Take Pat for example. She had come to me to learn to ask Spirit. She said she was distrustful of her coworkers. She worried someone was going to, in her words, "Stab me in the back." Although she liked her job, she didn't like feeling she was going to get into trouble. When I asked Spirit about her situation, I heard the word "systemic." Spirit revealed an image of an infection, and I at once sensed that what I was seeing was infected throughout. I was able to relate it to Pat's situation. I explained that Spirit was saying she was not alone, many people at her job felt the same way—they did not trust the people around them. This was a way bigger workplace issue than just Pat; it was a problem that started small and spread like a disease.

When I explained this to her, she agreed wholeheartedly. Spirit wanted her to stop looking at it as just *her* problem and instead see it as a cultural problem and tackle it from that angle. Since Pat was in a leadership position within the company, she was able to leave our conversation with a sense of purpose about how she could create a safer environment for all.

While all this "just ask Spirit" stuff may seem confusing from time to time, I want you to know that *each time you focus on the moment, what is happening right here and right now, you are showing up for Spirit.* I've learned that all emotional processing happens in the now and all Spirit connections happen in the now. While it can be tempting to start your day checking your texts or answering your e-mails, taking a moment to go within—whether a deep breath, walking outside, meditating, reading something meaningful, or prayer—I encourage you to create space for Spirit.

SIGNS THAT YOU'RE SHOWING UP

- You take things less personally, seeing situations as part of the lessons your soul is here to learn.
- You know you come from something greater than you.
- You know you are better off feeling than resisting your emotions.
- You ask Spirit before you respond to any major decisions.
- You take time to offer thanks and praise.
- You see external feedback (signs, synchronicities) as validation for your inner knowing.

SOUL

Once you show up and ask, then you need to *listen* to Spirit. After I'd finished an interview on my podcast, my guest reached out to me and asked if I wanted to cowrite a book. She was a well-known author who had excellent credentials and a great track record for book sales. My first response was "Yes!" We went back and forth for a while exchanging ideas and titles, but as time went on, I started having second thoughts. On paper, we were a terrific match. Each of us had over twenty years of experience, masters' degrees in mental health, excellent work ethics, as well as a solid understanding of the book industry. Yet something inside me told me this was not the avenue to take, at least not at this time.

I was having difficulty knowing the difference between whether I was feeling overwhelmed or guided by Spirit. I took myself through a Cleanse, sat in meditation for a few minutes, and then wrote down on a piece of paper: *Spirit, tell me more.* Then I paused. Within seconds a flash of an image of a dead-end street sign popped into my mind. Right after the image of the dead-end street sign, an image of a wall popped into my mind. I've found Spirit will often present things two or three ways so I fully get the message. At this point, I knew I had a choice: follow what I saw in my mind's eye, or override what I saw (i.e., ignore my intuition or Spirit) and do it anyway.

Here's what I've learned about decision-making: if something is really meant to be in your life, it will circle back to you. So often our soul's journey is about timing. Yet when we live predominately as human beings rather than spiritual beings in a human body, we treat letting go or saying no as a nerve-racking experience. We worry more about what the other person will think or whether we are making a mistake than we do about keeping our energy in flow. Saying, "No, thank you," to my friend was less about shutting an opportunity down and more about placing more attention on what I was letting in. I e-mailed my friend and let her know I was going to focus on writing *Just Ask Spirit* instead. Now that I was no longer trying to focus on two things, the energy for this one thing—this book—came flooding in.

When I asked Spirit to teach me more about the soul, I heard four words with distinct pauses in between each: *avenue . . . road . . . path . . . journey.*

When you overthink or analyze your situation (like I was doing in the case of considering working with another author), you are operating with limited data. To look at it another way, your mind is fantastic at digging up past experiences, comparing, or imagining the future. What the mind does not do very well, at least without proper training, is connecting you to your soul.

Your soul is highly intelligent. It contains a deeper understanding of all that is. As theosophist and writer Alice Bailey put it, "The Soul is the self-shining from within" (*Esoteric Psychology 1*, p. 130). If you've ever said something like "I feel it in my soul" or "This feeds my soul," you know what I mean. When you feel something in your soul, it lights you up. When you choose to go about your life from a place of meaning (rather than external appearances), you activate your light (soul) and Spirit (consciousness).

In Buddhist philosophy, there is no soul or self; these are simply constructs of the *I* made up by the mind. When it came to Spirit, Buddha encouraged his followers to *experience* Spirit rather than put a context around it. In other words, you may experience yourself as the *I* or the *me*. For example, I may think of myself as "I am Sherianna Boyle, an author, mother, wife, and spiritual teacher." Yet, if I take those titles away, I have to ask, *Who am I?* Remove the labels, ego identity, constructs (control from the left hemisphere of your brain), and you become one with the universe.

As the information and guidance comes in from Spirit, the attachments to ego, identity, and outcome loosen. It's important to be prepared for this! Otherwise, it can be a major hiccup. The thing is, people are afraid of letting go of these labels, mainly because we've become so accustomed to functioning within them. At one point, I couldn't figure out the significance of my life, and I became depressed. It wasn't until I started to process my emotions that my attachments to needing to know started to change. Instead, I focused on ways I could make my life meaningful.

Again, it's not just me. I've seen many people focused on their identity. They care more about how the world sees them (rich, young, pretty, successful, popular) than they do about experiencing their feelings. This puts them on a treadmill of trying to keep up with this fabricated version of ourselves. Here's the thing: You don't become good enough, you *are* good enough, and most importantly, your emotions are enough. As Alice Baily first wrote, in 1936, "Men will know, and know soon, that the soul is not an imaginary fiction, that it is just a symbolic way of expressing a deep-seated hope and is not man's method of building a defense mechanism; nor is it an illusion way of escape from a distressing present. They will know that a soul is a Being, a Being that is responsible for all that appears on the phenomenal planet" (*Esoteric Psychology*, p. 109).

Yet without creating space to feel, it can become easy to attach to quick fixes and outcomes as a way to manage the stress of the moment. Rather than *have* an experience, we try to control that experience. This is what happened when I thought about doing the project with my author friend. I immediately started

> Rather than have an experience, we try to control that experience.

to weigh the pros and cons, map out the steps, and forecast the result, instead of asking (inviting) Spirit in for guidance. By choosing to ask Spirit, I was choosing to be simultaneously present to what was happening in that moment. While our project might have turned out fine, things always tend to go more smoothly when you are aligned with Spirit.

The mind can become quite the enabler.

Your mind can be great at rehashing the past, making up excuses, minimizing intuition, and maximizing insecurity. This is because the mind takes you away from feeling and presence. If you are in fear or feel blocked, it's especially important for you to invite Spirit in. This allows you to be better equipped to trust the next steps, phase, or chapter of your soul path.

Although nowadays we tend to use the word "soul" only when it comes to human beings, philosopher and mathematician Pythagoras (ca 580–500 BC). He believed in animism, that humans and other creatures had souls. This was a metaphysical belief called *animism*. Other people have described soul as "living being" or "to breathe." Which brings us back to feeling. While it may seem like what you feel is influenced by what is happening around you, the soul reminds us that we have history and some of our present-day emotions may be much older than we think.

SOUL HISTORY

You have a human history, which includes your physical development, experiences, and memories in your current physical body, as well as a soul history, which is the evolution of the nonphysical part of you. The physical part of you is measured in time while the nonphysical is timeless. Much information about the soul has been gathered through therapies such as past-life regression. American psychiatrist Brian L. Weiss, MD, author of *Many Lives, Many Masters*, states through therapies such as past-life regression, in which you get in touch with your past experiences, you can learn more about where your soul has traveled, the lessons, learnings, and encounters you have endured, and that this can strengthen your relationship with yourself and others today.

One of the best parts of asking Spirit is that Spirit considers your entire soul history. What I learned through Cleansing is this happens through the breath. Your inhale and your exhale are great storytellers. Through my work I have witnessed the timelessness of the breath, how it has the capacity to move through all barriers giving you access to both the subconscious and conscious mind.

By connecting and asking Spirit (remember, this is an invitation), you are simultaneously giving yourself permission to fully process not just the emotions of today but also throughout your existence. How cool is that!

SOUL	SPIRIT
Has memory/history	Pure, life-force energy
Contains experiences, wisdom	Helps you carry out the guidance and wisdom
Travels, timeless	Connects to Source
Chooses	Guides
Anchors	Moves
Knows	Trusts

Furthermore, here are how emotions and Spirit are alike. Both:
- Affect how we feel and act
- Play a role in our well-being and how we relate to ourselves and others
- Can be a source of motivation, healing, and inspiration
- Impact our happiness and relationships
- Can be experienced through the senses

- Can be suppressed and oppressed
- Are impacted by our beliefs, judgments, and expectations
- Can bring us balance, inner strength, and resiliency
- Help you connect to something greater than yourself
- Are timeless, infinite in nature

As your emotions move by way of Cleanse and other exercises in this book, you'll come to see how they generate energy. This means the vibrations they carry increase in speed, what we call *energetic frequency*. This is what I call *energy is in action* or states of manifesting. To manifest means to bring something from the nonphysical into the physical. For example, when you ask Spirit to help you increase your finances, you are choosing to activate the abundant nature and infinite potential within. You might recall that in the beginning of this book, I mentioned your purpose is to get to know yourself. When you ASK for things like good health, love, and happiness you are in essence choosing to call forth or remember those qualities and capabilities that already exist in you. As my guides have shared with me, when we feel a sense of lack and ask to manifest, it is a sign we are trying to remember ourselves as abundant, infinite beings.

Therefore, when you speak to Spirit, it can help to ask Spirit to call forth the part of you that *is* as opposed to the part that *wants* things such as abundance, love, companionship, resolution, and more. The way we do this via the Cleanse is in the final step, "E," when you recite "I am" statements.

Now that you've taken time to understand Spirit and soul, let's take a deeper dive into the emotional part. Learning more about what emotions are, how they work, and the way they help you ask Spirit will prepare you for meeting your spiritual team in Chapter 4.

CLEANSE HIGHLIGHT

C, Clear Reactivity

In step one of Cleanse, you are calming your nervous system down through mindful tools such as breathing, visualizing light, and gentle stretches. This helps you to:

- Connect to your higher self
- Tone your vagus nerve
- Become centered and grounded
- Reduce stress and promote a sense of safety
- Circulate the breath and support the flow of energy

I'll delve into this in Part 2, and you'll practice them in Part 3, but for now, doing something simple like sitting up tall, relaxing your shoulders as you drop your right ear toward your right shoulder (to stretch your neck) for five seconds, and then taking your head back to the center and doing the opposite side (left ear toward your left shoulder) can be a way to release tension and calm your body (and mind) down.

CHAPTER 2

THE SPIRIT
OF EMOTIONS

*Not all emotions need to be or benefit from
being verbalized. Some become recognized,
released, and transformed through the consciousness
of bodily movement and breath.*

I was in a yoga studio getting ready to teach a two-hour work-
shop on Cleanse when I overheard a conversation between the front
desk person and one of the women who was attending. Apparently,
the woman was trying to pay, but her credit card kept being declined.
The front desk person told her she could pay later, but the woman
turned down the offer and left the building. I was guided to go out to

my car to retrieve an item I had brought for class. As I was reaching into the backseat I looked over and saw the woman crying in her car. I approached her window and asked if she was okay. She replied, "I'm fine. I'm just taking it as a sign from Spirit." I walked away wondering, *Was that* really *Spirit or her triggered emotions?*

My feeling is that it wasn't Spirit, it was a trigger. As you might have guessed already there is a pretty significant difference between the two. Triggers are unconscious and conscious memories. Often evoked by unprocessed strong emotions like fear, triggers have been known to take you out of the present moment and into the fight, flight, fear, or freak-out response. While the memory attached to the emotion may not always surface during a triggering episode, the feeling or remembrance of something being bad, wrong, or scary may.

You know it's a trigger because it always causes you to turn to a cycle of thinking. In the brain this can look like overthinking, analyzing, controlling, and predicting as a means to get out (flee) or control (freeze, fight) the experience. This is a protective mechanism based on the body's survival mode. The challenge is that this way of functioning does extraordinarily little for you in terms of emotional processing, leaving you further disconnected from your true power and Spirit.

When I teach, I notice that one of the ways triggers regularly show up is that people start comparing themselves to others. In other words, rather than be in the experience, they judge the experience and others. Yet here are two things I want you to keep in mind:

- Triggers are not emotions; they are reactions.
- Triggers are not your truths; they are bodily feedback (information) trying to let you know you have an old (suppressed or repressed) emotion that needs to be processed.

When you don't treat triggers in this way, that is, process them, they can take on a life of their own, creating repeating patterns and cycles of reactivity. On the outside these may look different (different people or situations), but on the inside, energetically, they resemble one another. When unrecognized or left untreated, recurring triggers can make you feel as if life is out of control. This may look or sound like: *I just need to get through this. . . . I have one more appointment and then . . . Once this is over I can . . .* Then before you know it, you find yourself moving further away from the one energy, state, consciousness that can bring you to back to oneness within seconds: Spirit.

Here's the thing: we humans like to control or manage what may be up ahead. It's a survival thing. We don't like unpleasant surprises (like our credit card being declined or a traffic jam). Yet my guides tell me when it comes to connecting and manifesting (yes, your guides can help you with this), a little element of surprise and embracing the unexpected (even when the credit card doesn't work) may be exactly the amount of discomfort you need in that moment. It's your discomfort that leads to growth and expansion. It's your discomfort that moves energy, and it's your discomfort (aka vulnerability) that can and will open you up to Spirit. *After all, isn't this how miracles happen?*

Yet, if you are busy trying to control everything, this just can't happen. Getting to know what emotions are, how they work, and the value they bring to our lives can help.

WHAT ARE EMOTIONS?

Emotion comes from the Latin word *emovere*, which means to move through. In terms of their anatomy, they have both physical and nonphysical forms of energy (vibration) in motion. On a physical level, emotions have a biochemical component. Neuroscientist, pharmacologist, and author Candace Pert, PhD, was one of the first to make the claim that emotions are a form of intercellular messengers called neuropeptides. She discusses her discoveries in the book *Molecules of Emotion*. Although her research initially set out to further develop pharmacology in this area, her work would take an unexpected turn into what became known as mind-body medicine.

According to the National Library of Medicine, neuropeptides impact things like:

- Cellular activity
- Bodily inflammation, circulation
- The awakening of senses

Here's the thing: We need emotions to be able to connect to one another and Spirit. If you think your guides don't experience emotions, think again. My guides tell me they have lots of them, yet as I mentioned in preface, the difference is they don't get stuck in them. This is because they don't have a physical body with a brain, which has been conditioned or programmed to analyze, control, manage, and figure out every energetic (emotional) movement like we do. The good news is that due to things like *neuroplasticity*—the ability of brain neurons to change and compensate when necessary, for example, after trauma—we know we can change our brains and be more like Spirit. Rather than react to energy, we can learn how to transform it in ways in which it can serve the greater good for all.

Through our personal intentions, devotions, practices, and respect for the energy of our emotions, it's possible to live freely as spiritual beings, even as we learn the lessons our soul came here to learn. My guides tell me we don't have to suffer to evolve. The exercises in this book will help.

EVERY EXPERIENCE IS DIFFERENT

Amy was a student in my Spirit class who contacted me to tell me she was at work one day, speaking to one of her clients, when she started experiencing a tingly sensation all over her body. As Amy was advising *her* client, she started to feel like the energy of Spirit was speaking through her. When she asked me what I thought might be happening, my response was "Don't overthink it. If it's truly helping someone, then let the information flow. If anything, slow down. My guides (this was me channeling as I was speaking to her) are telling me when you get information you start to talk fast."

"Oh my God, Sherianna, yes, I totally do that. People always tell me I talk fast, but I never considered it could be related to Spirit."

Here's what I know: while information from Spirit can come in fast, this doesn't mean you have to talk fast. With that said, don't feel bad about it if this happens; instead, see it as a sign that you are connected. You may speed up or talk more slowly. See what you notice about yourself.

What I have learned is the more you take time to process your emotions, the easier it will be for you to hold onto the information that comes in through Spirit. Emotional processing trains your mind and body to stay calm. When you are calm, you have an easier time concentrating. This helps you keep your boundaries in check, meaning you are less likely to speak quickly or overshare.

The good news is either way you win. By choosing to open to Spirit, you'll likely be more comfortable with your emotions. Conversely, by choosing to process your emotions, this will naturally lead to becoming closer and more proficient at connecting to Spirit. Either way, the catalyst is often genuine curiosity or a need (perhaps after a significant loss) to learn more about emotions, energy, intuition, and Spirit.

What I've learned is that this curiosity is often little nudges from your Spirit guides pointing you in the exact direction you need to go at that point in your life. These little directions can often be early signs of new chapters, learnings, friendships, endeavors, experiences, opportunities, and more. Trust that when you allow your emotions to be processed, they will give you the clarity and confidence you need to trust your path ahead. Without a doubt, part of the pathway will include learning how to navigate the energy of your emotions without fear or resistance.

THE ENERGY OF EMOTIONS

Think of emotions like running water. The less the water moves, the worse the water quality becomes. When water stagnates, it becomes a breeding ground for bacteria and toxins. Since the human body is more than 60 percent water, a lack of circulation contributes negatively to your overall mood and mental health. As Dr. Candace Pert explained, emotions impact circulation, your immune system, and physical health: In her book *Molecules of Emotion*, she states, "Emotions. The neuropeptides and receptors, the biochemicals of emotion, are the messengers carrying information to link the major systems of the body into one unit that we can call the bodymind" (p. 189).

When it comes to moving the energy of your emotions, it's important to note that you are not getting rid of your emotions—no, no, no! Let's not throw the baby out with the bathwater. Remember they connect you to consciousness (Spirit). What you are releasing through increasing circulation and vibrational frequency are *reactions*.

REACTIVITY

In my book *Emotional Detox: 7 Steps to Release Toxicity & Energize Joy*, I define "reactivity" as the way we make the uncomfortable comfortable.

One of the ways to know if you are in reactivity (also known as being triggered) is you may be focusing more on what is happening outside you than inside. For example, the woman in the yoga studio was focused on the fact that her credit card was not working. In that moment she had a choice: move through those emotions of discomfort, or manage them by doing something quickly, like leaving. While I always encourage you to do what *feels* right, sometimes you have to ask yourself: *Is this really a state of feeling, or am I being triggered?*

If it takes you away from the now—this moment—it was likely a trigger. Spirit and emotional processing can bring you back into the present. Sometimes we go into reactivity because we showed up already in a depleted state. In other words, you just might not have enough energy to work through whatever is showing up in your life. Perhaps this is why our spiritual guides (more on who they are in the next chapter) are always encouraging us to take better care of ourselves and our energy. They know that in order to grow, learn, create, and expand, self-care and self-compassion are essential.

Without emotions in flow, you are more likely to numb your emotions through reactions, such as chronic thinking, worrying, and ruminating, than you are to run them. When you learn how to let emotions flow this makes learning how to receive the energy of Spirit easier. As a result, your ability to connect to Spirit will become like second nature.

Along the way, it's important to pause and look at how far you have come. If you've ever looked back at your life and said to yourself: *I am not sure how I did that. How did I work two jobs and raise a child? How did I move through an eating disorder? How did I get out of an abusive relationship? How did I recover from substance abuse or a divorce? How did I earn that degree?* Then it's likely you know how powerful these simple reflections can be.

Yet here is where this book is different from any of the other ones I've written. Once you get the idea of what Cleansing looks and feels like, then the next step is to teach you other ways you can get to know the energy of your emotions, and that is through your *psychic senses.*

PSYCHIC SENSES

Four of the psychic senses are *clairvoyance, clairsentience, clairaudience,* and *claircognizance.* Each one is described below. Keep in mind they all contain a spectrum of abilities, and the more you process emotions, the more consistent and reliable these psychic senses will be. As with physical and psychological development, your psychic senses can be influenced by genetics, environment, diet, trauma and other experiences, and more.

CLAIRVOYANCE, CLAIRSENTIENCE, CLAIRAUDIENCE, CLAIRCOGNIZANCE

Clairvoyance or Clear Seeing: A person who has clear seeing may have an extra ability to see images, colors, or visions of future events. For example, they might see in their mind's eye assorted colors and shapes when their emotions are in a state of processing and/or they are picking up on Spirit.

Clairsentience or Clear Feeling: This is the ability to feel or sense spirits. It can also be used to describe the ability to get a "gut feeling" about someone or something. This can help you make decisions or lead to powerful insight (like Amy) without having much evidence. Emotions can also show up as a "gut" feeling, perhaps a pit in your stomach or moment of uneasiness. The key is to let the energy move and the clarity will come.

Clairaudience or Clear (Psychic) Hearing: This is being able to hear spirits . . . and I am going to go out on a limb here and say you can also hear emotions. Sometimes a word like "humiliation" will pop into my mind when I work with a client, letting me know which emotion needs to be moved. This psychic sense can also be that you pick up on music or sounds from a source that is not noticeable to the normal ear. As you move your emotions and develop this sense, you may receive a message (word, phrase) indicating there has been an energetic shift inside you. See this as a positive sign; you are connecting.

Claircognizance or Clear Knowing: The difference between claircognizance and clairvoyance is that you have no images or visions; you just *know*, even without prior knowledge or evidence. With emotions sometimes you know something with zero evidence. Lean into what you feel without judgment and ask Spirit to tell you more. For example, "Tell me more about this feeling of knowing."

While your psychic senses are not limited to the four types just explained, they can certainly take you beyond the "normal" experience, and they can be a wonderful place to start exploring your emotions in new ways. I believe once children are beyond the age of ten or eleven, we ought to be teaching these higher senses for exploring their emotions to better prepare them for the world.

Let's take a moment here to identify how you take in the energy of emotions. For example, when it comes to picking up on your emotions or other people's (maybe your best friend or child), how do you receive this information? Using the chart information as a guide, write in the space below.

_____

_____

_____

_____

_____

_____

- Now do the same with Spirit. Ask yourself, when it comes to picking up on the energy of Spirit (maybe a loved one in Spirit or a holy being or angel), which psychic sense do you rely on to receive the information that they are around you?
- Finally, when you're having trouble connecting to the higher realms, how do you know? What sense feels blocked? If something feels blocked, then it's likely you know what it feels like when it's unblocked. This might be one of the senses you want to pay attention to. For example, if you are distracted, this may be a sign your clear seeing is blocked. When our minds are all over the place, we no longer are present to what is around us. Write your insights in a journal or below.

_____

_____

_____

_____

_____

_____

As I told my student Amy, I don't want you to split hairs here, meaning don't try to figure out what is an emotion and what is Spirit. This is because—I'll say it here and likely say it again later—*it is all one.* Think in terms of something called the Spiritual Law of Oneness: There is no separation, everything is one, and when we detach ourselves from this oneness, we suffer. Everything happens at the same time—like emotional processing, spirit, and healing. The key is to learn how to raise your vibration, so you don't get overstimulated, bogged down, or overwhelmed during the process. Finding quiet times of your day (maybe early morning) to connect to be present to yourself can help.

EMOTIONS AND THE BRAIN

It was no accident when Jeff Tarrant, author of *Becoming Psychic: Lessons from the Minds of Mediums, Healers and Psychics,* along with psychic medium and Spirit artist Maria Forland were guests on the *Just Ask Spirit* podcast. At the time, I was in the final stages of writing this book. Spirit had been nudging me to contact Maria. Another sign that it is Spirit acting is when you are thinking about someone or something and you don't know why.

When I did contact Maria, she told me she would be happy to be on my show and asked if I would consider including her dear friend Jeff Tarrant. What I didn't know at the time, but later learned, is Jeff had been studying the brains of psychic mediums for quite some time using devices such as EEG (electroencephalogram). I felt like Spirit pretty much handed me the research.

The full episode of our discussion can be found in the *Just Ask Spirit* podcast archives (Sept. 4, 2024). Here is a little bit that Jeff said about the brain, psychic development, and emotions:

There are a couple of regions in the brain that are involved in that aspect of connection to others, these are also areas of the brain that often show up with mediumship. One of them is the right parietal lobe also called the "God spot" when that part of the brain becomes interrupted (via things like meditation), so that it is not able to do its normal job (which is to control or separate), our boundaries become more open, and our ability to take in other people's perspectives, and to empathize becomes increased. Our ability to connect to something outside of ourselves increases as well.

Another part of the brain called the insula has a lot to do with emotion. This area of the brain lights up during compassion meditation and empathic activities. These two regions on the right side of the brain seem to be connected to emotions. When mediums are doing their work connecting to Spirit, we see these same areas light up.

These findings validated what I and so many of my clients were experiencing; emotional freedom is possible when you choose to develop your relationship with Spirit. It is then you can get to know yourself as an energetic being, capable of taking in and moving energy in powerful ways.

ENERGY, PSYCHOLOGY, AND MEDICINE

Tools and strategies that are mindful in nature are like *spiritual* medicine. Certainly, this doesn't mean you no longer see your doctor and get regular checkups; what it does mean is you no longer have to limit yourself to the resources available on Earth. There are a whole slew of doctors in the Spirit realm, like Archangel Raphael, whose name means "God heals," who can also assist you in your journey.

I refer to archangels throughout the book.
Different people relate to them in different ways, but
I define them as messengers of God.

As the fields of energy psychology and energy medicine continue to grow as an additional means for treating disorders like addiction, anxiety, and depression, more and more people will become comfortable getting to know their *energy body* (the undercurrents of energy that travel through the body or the body of energy within our bodies) and *energy field* (how energy travels outside the body, sometimes called an aura) as a resource for transformation, healing, and Spirit connection.

Through the study of energy (emotions) you get to explore the unknown, that is, what you can't see, the invisible energy lines called *meridians*. You learn that keeping a strong field of energy around the body (your aura) serves you. I'll teach you how to work with meridians as lines in a road map from the crown of your head to the soles of your feet.

I'll go into detail in Chapter 3, when I discuss chakras (areas of the body where energy pools), but until then, know there are twelve major meridians in the body, which are connected in a network, branching out into organs, glands, and primary parts of the body. Each meridian is associated with specific emotional and behavioral characteristics. For example, the heart meridian may be associated with heartbreak. The governing meridian that runs up the center of your body from your lower back, over the top of your head, and beneath your nose is associated with confidence and courage. The stomach meridian is about developing trust and releasing worry.

While this can be a lot to take in, the point is to show you how compatible and alike emotions and Spirit really are. Each one is experienced as electromagnetic energy. When this energy is in motion, your level of awareness or consciousness increases.

I once guided a client (well, it wasn't me; it was Spirit working through me) in a practice. The intention was to teach her how to let go of mental override or push, go beyond her triggers, and surrender to Spirit. It's called the "Ha" exercise.

"Ha"

Find a comfortable seated position. It's best to try it for the first time while sitting in a chair, feet flat on the floor. Be sure your spine is nice and long. As you inhale, reach your arms overhead with your fingers loose. While your arms are overhead, make fists with both hands, and then pull your arms back down with an audible exhalation of a *ha* sound. Repeat this, lifting your arms on the inhale, and exhaling making the *ha* sound. *Inhale, ha, inhale, ha, inhale, ha . . .*

Move at your own pace. The point of this exercise is not to do it fast but rather to show you how much you do things from your mental mind. Notice how the mental mind will push you, tell you to keep going while your Spirit will encourage you to let go. Lift and lower the arms for anywhere between one to three minutes straight until you surrender to your Spirit.

This exercise can show you how Spirit doesn't just come from above; it comes from within. Ask yourself where you got your strength to let go? Very often people report feeling the strength of Spirit coming down from above through their crown, as well as from beneath them, as if rising from Mother Earth.

Once while doing this exercise, I released my mental mind (lowered my arms) and just took in the moment. I felt so light yet grounded at the same time. It was then I heard the word "atman," not knowing what it meant. When I looked it up later, I discovered it was a Hindu word meaning essence or soul.

According to the American Psychological Association, "Emotions are conscious mental reactions (such as anger or fear) usually directed toward a specific object and typically accompanied by physiological and behavioral changes in the body." Yet it's through mindful practices such as the previous ones and through Cleanse that I've learned these conscious mental reactions can be transformed into a new experience. When emotions are no longer directed *at* a certain thing, person, situation, or inward, they can be transmuted *into* the energy of direction, that is, inner guidance, from Spirit. When you are able to make this simple shift from "at" direction to "into" direction, you are no longer separate from your emotions or spirit. All it takes is *ninety seconds.*

NINETY SECONDS

I had the privilege of interviewing neuroanatomist and Harvard brain scientist Jill Bolte Taylor, PhD, twice on the *Just Ask Spirit* podcast. When she told me it takes ninety seconds to process an emotion, I wasn't surprised. First, because I had read her book *My Stroke of Insight* several times, and second, I knew from the experience of practicing Cleanse on myself that I had often felt that by the third step of the Cleanse, *E* for emit, I was in a quite different state from when I had started.

Dr. Taylor explains that when a person has a reaction to something in their environment, "There's a ninety-second chemical process that happens in the body; after that, any remaining emotional response is just the person choosing to stay in that emotional loop." In other words, if you're still feeling anger or disappointment, it's because you're allowing yourself to continue to be angry and disappointed.

In many ways, making a choice to Cleanse helps you carve out new neuropathways. Similar to creating a new path in the woods, the more you walk that route, the smoother and clearer it will be. You'll begin to recognize how it feels to move from reactivity to feeling, and as this occurs, you'll get better at trusting, listening, and knowing what is and is not Spirit. This will clarify how you invite, ask, and receive the benefits of Spirit.

As the Spirit within you becomes stronger, asking Spirit won't just be about finding answers but also about discovering a way to bring stability, peace, and harmony to yourself and others. Soon you'll discover the love and respect your spiritual team carries. Let's get to know them now.

CLEANSE HIGHLIGHT: L LOOK INWARD

The purpose of step two, L look inward, is both to acknowledge and move the energy of your emotions by responding to the stem sentences with an inhale (inflate lower abdomen slowly for the count of three . . . one . . . two . . . three . . .) then holding your breathing gently at the top for one count, and then exhaling three, two, one. When you breathe imagine you are responding as your higher self (Spirit). It's as if your spiritual self is saying out loud, *How I feel in my body right now is . . . inhale . . . exhale. . . .*

Then move to the next stem sentence, for example: *When I am fully connected to my higher self, it makes me feel . . . inhale . . . exhale. . . . Consciously connecting to my Spirit now makes me feel . . . inhale . . . exhale. . . .* After three or four stem sentences and breaths, move to step three, Emit.

CHAPTER 3

HOW DOES IT WORK?

*Pay less attention to how much you have to do
and more to the pace you go about doing it.*

"So, what would you like to focus on today? How can I help you?"
I asked my client.

"My sister went to you, and you channeled her messages from
Spirit. I have a few friends who have died and would like a message."

Oh boy . . . here we go again. Like I said earlier, I don't consider
myself a psychic medium. If you have ever been to either, you know
they all have their own way of connecting to Spirit. I've seen some
psychics connect by rocking back and forth, others recite a prayer
and call in their spiritual guides, some have you pull a few angel

cards, or ask to hold something with your energy on it like your car keys. Instead, I will most likely guide you through a Cleanse to get the energy of your emotions (and mine) flowing and connecting that way so that you can receive them— sometimes with my help.

Trained psychics have often been taught either directly or indirectly the ability to move their energy from a high frequency (beta) brain wave state, where you are alert, into more alpha (lower frequency) states, where creative, daydreamy, intuitive states can be accessed. While it is nice to think I have a special gift, what teaching Cleanse has taught me is *we all* have these abilities in some form. It's not a matter of whether you have "the gift" but more so how much practice you have in learning how to work with it. Now I'm not saying some people don't have a stronger ability than others. I've interviewed many psychics whose previous experiences (either through their genetics or past lives) seemed to greatly enhance their abilities. But what I am saying is that your emotions are a resource for developing your intuition.

"How about this," I suggested to my client, "let's start your energy—emotions—moving, and then I can ask Spirit if there is anything like energy blockages, beliefs, or old traumas preventing you from receiving messages from your loved ones in spirit." It didn't surprise me that she would really be into that idea. Most people want to be able to connect themselves but aren't sure how.

Here is the way I see it: when my client and I move through a Cleanse together, it's as if we're both hooking up to the same radio station. I like to refer to it as Higher Self Network. Sure, at first it may seem like I'm tuning in, and they really aren't sure what station they are dialing into, yet, with practice, they learn (as you will) and it becomes quite natural. Think of it like an assembly line: it takes connection, communication, practice, and skill development to get the rhythm and flow in place.

This is exactly how I would like *you* to think about the process as you move through the pages and practices in this book. By choosing to process what you feel, you are moving out of beta (alert) states into alpha (calm) states. While I have never measured the changes in frequencies, I don't really need to—I can feel it.

Helané Wahbeh, ND, MCR, author of *The Science of Channeling*, has researched this area thoroughly. In her book she states, "Studies do make it pretty clear that a person's state of awareness is essential for channeling. Usually, some form of an altered state of consciousness (ASC) supports channeling experiences" (p. 97). One of those altered states of consciousness available to all is meditation. When it comes to the next two steps of the Cleanse, *A* for activate and *N* for nourish, think of it as similar to meditation.

After combing through Helané Wahbeh's research, what became clear once again is the striking similarities between what we do with our emotions and the way we tune into Spirit. For example, just like we can develop defensive mechanisms for protecting rather than processing our emotions, we can also create defensive mechanisms around channeling.

Time and time again, I've witnessed this in myself and so many clients. For example, you might pick up on the energy of Spirit (as if tuned to a particular radio station). It may feel unfamiliar, strange or even anxiety provoking, so in order to cope with what we are picking up on, like

> Just like we can develop defensive mechanisms for protecting rather than processing our emotions, we can also create defensive mechanisms around channeling.

emotions, we turn to our thoughts (for example, analyze) as a way to manage the energy. I wonder if unconsciously or consciously we do this because we know thinking will distract us from what we feel. The challenge is this way of responding also leaves the impression (some people call it an illusion) that whatever we were picking up on is gone. Yet we know from Albert Einstein that energy doesn't go away—you can't destroy it; however, consciousness (awareness) does.

You see, what happens is, as you connect to Spirit, your electromagnetic energy can increase. This can at times (but not always) elevate your heart rate a bit or bring about some nervousness. Having this discomfort might remind you of other times in your life when you felt anxious or fearful, so inevitably you may choose to shut the energy (sensations) down by distracting yourself with your thoughts.

The same kind of reaction can happen with your emotions. If you are not familiar with feeling them at first, it may make you feel uncomfortable, uneasy, or vulnerable. As a result, you might get nervous and unconsciously choose to shut your emotions down by talking too much, running your thoughts, or becoming close-minded. Keep in mind this is not to be confused with being in a situation where you sense danger. That is completely different, and in that case, you should trust what you feel and protect yourself. What I'm speaking about asking Spirit is far more than noticing signs and asking questions; it is also a journey of personal development and awakening of unrealized potential.

Spiritual teachers on earth and in the Spirit realms have shown us time and time again that with proper guidance and tools, *your* Spirit has the ability to contribute great things. Yet part of the process will be learning to get out of your own way and relinquish your ego. As stated in ancient Indian text, *The Dhammapada:*

For the personal ego, which seems so real and considers its satisfactions so all-important, this does not add up to an attractive self-image. The bundle of thoughts, memories, desires, fears, urges, anxieties, and aspirations that we think of ourselves is largely an illusion: a lot of separation mental events temporarily associated with a physical body, but nothing that anyone can call whole (*The Dhammapada*, p. 82).

How does it work? By turning inward to discover your I, you transcend your roles, identities, and attachments. It's your I minus the labeling of your emotions as good or bad, or spirits as good or bad, your I and your unlimited potential as an energetic being. Asking Spirit is not about getting the right answers or delivering the perfect message. Ask for whatever you want; Spirit will never judge you. Just keep in mind that a large part of what makes asking Spirit most effective is having an open heart and a powerful sense of I—not as separate but rather connected to something greater. When I channel for a client or for myself, my ego (the "me" part of me), defensiveness, fear, competitiveness must step out of the way, and the I part of me has to step forward. You'll see in Chapter 15 how important it is for you to establish your I when asking.

Should fear, worry, or doubt creep in, it will be spiritual practices such as the ones in this book—reciting verses (like the previous ones), visualizing white light, imagining an infinity sign above your head, Cleansing, journaling, meditating—that can guide you back to being and your intention.

SETTING INTENTIONS

I used to get caught up and even fearful of what and who I may be channeling. Was I bringing something bad or evil into my life?

Taking myself through a Cleanse practice before communicating or asking Spirit has helped tremendously. The Cleanse has a way of grounding your energy into the present moment where anxiety cannot exist. Don't worry, this is what I'll teach you. As anxiety dissipates, your sense of I increases.

When it comes to asking Spirit, the clearer you are around your goals and intentions, the better your spiritual team can assist you. Think of it like going to a restaurant. When you place an order for a sandwich, you specify what kind of sandwich. If you are unsure of what you want, you may send mixed signals. In other words, if what you think, feel, and know intuitively is not fully aligned, one might cancel out the other vibrationally. I may think I want to connect to Spirit, but a part of me might feel ambivalent or doubtful.

Your spiritual team knows and reads your energy. Just as you can tell the difference between someone's hollow words and when their actions reflect those words. This is very much how Spirit works; only instead of actions, it's vibrations. Spirit is more likely to respond when you are fully aligned, that is, when what you say and feel, your vibrations or energy, match.

This is because you have free will (more on this later in the chapter). Therefore, if you are choosing to focus on your perceived problems or obstacles, Spirit will not stop you. They may send you messages (like numbers, a flash of light, or feathers in unusual places) to catch your attention, calm your nerves, and set your mind in a new direction, but they will not directly interfere. I find these moments of insecurity are great opportunities to *ask* for help.

With that said, many people use the terms *goals* and *intentions* interchangeably, but my guides are telling me to teach you otherwise. Goals, they say, help you plan and project out into the future. When you take a moment to write them down (for example, to complete a college degree, exercise more regularly, or save money for a new car), goals are beneficial for helping you come up with a step-by-step plan for how to achieve them.

Intentions, on the other hand, are not about the future. They connect you to the energy (Spirit) of your goals in the present moment. For example, I may have a goal of writing a new book. When I choose (free will) to get up at 5 AM to write for two hours, I am living with intention. I no longer hope to write a book or want to complete a book (goal); I am the consciousness/Spirit of book writing. While the physical aspect of book writing may stop, the consciousness or the energy of what I am creating goes on. It lives within me, just as your intentions live within you. I believe that's because intentions are connected to your soul. Have you ever been drawn to something and aren't sure where your passion or drive comes from? What makes one person go for something while another person might sit idle? Perhaps it has something to do with overlapping goals and intentions.

You see, while goals set you in a certain direction, intentions may feel like a deep desire. Not unlike suppressed emotions, when you push them away or ignore them, it can feel like your Spirit is fading. You may have a goal to decrease stress in your life, which leads to living in intention as you take a walk in nature.

You may have a goal of going to the gym, yet it won't be until you are in the gym, experiencing the sounds of the weights clanging or the sensation of the treadmill under your feet, that you will be in the *energy* of intention. The same goes for Spirit. You can say you want to have a closer relationship with your team, and call on Spirit for help, yet it won't be until you are calling on your spiritual team that you'll be living with intention. Goals have a beginning and an end, while the intention of Spirit lives on. My guides tell me this is how we obtain *soul memory*.

If you go overboard with your goals—perhaps you have a tendency to be a perfectionist, or maybe you set very high expectations—kindly and gently guide yourself back to intention. Know that spiritual practices such as visualizing a pillar of white light moving through you from above your head, taking a deep inhale, and chanting the sound *hum* on exhale can keep you from overexerting mental energy. Intention is a state of cultivating and conserving energy/consciousness. Goals, on the other hand, may get you to exert more energy than you take in if you are not careful. Yet, here is the interesting part, the clearer you are about your goals and having intention alongside them, the less energy you will lose.

INTENTIONS IN ACTION

I worked with a client who had to have a difficult conversation with a fellow employee. I asked her what her goal was. She said she wanted to provide constructive feedback to the employee in a way that they would receive it in a positive manner.

"Can you imagine yourself," I asked, "speaking respectfully to this person, and can you imagine this person making contact with you, listening, and taking in what they are hearing?"

"Yes," she replied, "I can visualize that."

"This is you living with intention."

By visualizing the situation, my client entered a state of presence. This is one of the advantages of practices like visualization—they help you align your energy with intention. This is because your brain does not know the difference between doing and visualizing. When you imagine engaging in a respectful tone and watching the other person receive it in a positive way, your brain and body believes it's happening. Goals are more active while intention tends to be more passive. This is a good thing; like masculine and feminine energy, they balance each other out.

Perhaps this is the reason why so few people keep their New Year's resolutions. They believe they have to be constantly doing something to make it happen. The reality is *doing* isn't *being*. You need goals to help carry out your dreams and desires, and you need intentions to recharge and elevate energy. If you're not sure what your goals or purpose is, then there lies another reason to call in your Spirit team. Your spiritual team is the energy of intention. They live and exist in the now. In other words, they don't say they are going to help or support you; they are helping and supporting you. They don't say they are going to protect you and offer healings; they are protecting and offering you healings. It's not whether they are or not, but more so if you are choosing to ask and receive their help.

How do you choose it? Experience—that is, process and feel— your emotions. As you move through this process, my guides want you to think of it like this:

Imagine a time in your life when you went through a transition. Maybe you attended a new school or started a new job. At first you may have felt overwhelmed and confused. Then after a while you adjusted, and the things you learned became second nature. Spirit wants you to know this is how it will be at first when you are learning to communicate with Spirit. It might be uncomfortable, strange, and even frustrating. You may think to yourself, *Am I doing this right? Is anybody hearing me?* Yet, with practice, these doubts and insecurities will dissipate and transform into states of confidence.

Right now, you may have a goal of completing this book. As you move through the Cleanses, write in your journal, meditate, or take Spirit walks knowing you will be living your intention. When you think of your loved ones that have passed, they too are living with intention. They are no longer trying to be happy, healthy, balanced, and wise. They *are* happy, healthy, balanced, and wise, just not in a physical form anymore. I'm hoping this all makes sense.

Before moving on, take a moment here to write down a goal.

My goal is _____.

Now, take a deep breath and live with intention. Visualize yourself accomplishing your goal. Your visualization is the Spirit of your intention.

DISCOVERING MEANING

Now that you're clear about intentions, the next step is to focus on meaning. In Helané Wahbeh's book *The Science of Channeling*, sociologist Hannah Gilbert states: "Identifying the 'source' from which you are channeling is not essential. My interests were not concerned with whether or not mediums could scientifically prove they were in contact with a real, interactive spirit world, but rather treated the spirit world as something *socially* real and meaningful" (p. 119).

To find meaning is to discover the value in whatever it is you are connecting to. Ask yourself, *How does connecting to Spirit add value into my life?* If you are not sure, then Chapter 5, "The Benefits of Asking Spirit," may help. Another way to find meaning is to become part of a spiritual group. This can be a church group, meditation class, or a virtual offering such as the Membership (a virtual circle and meditation) I lead each week through my website, sheriannaboyle.com. When I asked the award-winning author of *The Intention Experiment*, Lynn McTaggart, what made her "power of eight" virtual groups so effective, she reported these three qualities: authenticity, being specific, and coming from the heart. These types of qualities can be nurtured and strengthened by becoming a part of a community of like-minded intentions.

You can also discover meaning through moments of stillness, quiet, or silence.

As you move through the Cleanse, you will notice after the *hum* or other sacred sounds such as *aad*—the sacred sound which represents "a return to source, the divine energy that exists in all things" (Lakshmi Sharma, Yoga)—this happens naturally. The *hum* mantra in Sanskrit stands for enlightenment. When I am receiving messages from Spirit, whether it is via journaling or meditating, I will often hum out loud one or two times to keep my Spirit connection strong. After the *hum*, I sit in silence for twenty seconds or so. I find chanting *hum* one or two times can bring the connection back.

Like when the audio on your computer doesn't work, this can happen with Spirit too. You see, this is how connecting with and asking Spirit works. You raise your vibration, and your spiritual team lowers theirs just enough so you can meet them in the middle.

When it comes to asking Spirit, this space of inner silence (as brief as it may be) serves as an important transition between feeling and processing and asking. The silence gives you a chance to take one more breath and to nurture the altruistic quality, which helps with recovery and healing.

Take a moment now to reflect and write down in the space that follows what Spirit means to you. How does asking Spirit bring value to your life? Exercises such as this help you build your awareness.

_____

_____

_____

_____

_____

AWARENESS

The spiritual laws of the universe teach us that what happens on the outside is often a result of what's happening on the inside. For example, low energy can cause us to feel overwhelmed and fatigued. As a result, you may become protective of your energy, stay home for a quiet evening on the couch rather than whoop it up with friends.

While vegging out in front of a movie may give you some much-needed downtime, it doesn't typically lead to emotional processing. It may calm you down and help you relax, but I'm not sure if chilling out will lead to any profound shifts in your energetic patterns, like living with awareness can. You need awareness to foster a sense of higher perception and knowing. Otherwise, you're more likely to slip into old patterns of reactivity.

The best thing that ever happened to me during my own Emotional Detox is that I didn't have enough energy to do the things that would normally take my mind off tasks like cleaning or watching television. At that time in my life everything felt like a trigger. Sounds, activity, people, you name it, it felt like no matter what I did I could not gain my sense of balance. The only thing I could do was ask Spirit. At the time I'm not sure what made me think of this, perhaps it was the energy of my guardian angel around me, but I chose to ask Spirit to show me how to process my emotions, not knowing this question would change my life.

From that point on, the steps of the Cleanse started to come through from states of awareness. At the time, I wasn't just in pain, I was very much aware of the pain. Rather than react to it, instead I reduced the reactivity by doing things such as reciting a mantra out loud such as *hum*, or the seed sounds (such as *lam*, *vam*) you will practice in the third step of the Cleanse: *E*, which stands for "Emit sound."

The word "emit" came to me one day when I had to contact my publisher about something. During that conversation, for whatever reason, I mentioned to the editor I was speaking with that I wanted step three to be a mantra, but I couldn't think of a word that began with *E* to represent it. Immediately, as if he knew it all along, he said, "Emit, use the word emit."

This is another example of how Spirit works—through other people. If you're having trouble with something, or Spirit wants you to pay attention to something, they might have someone say it to you. Have you ever had a stranger say something to you in a way that made you wonder how they knew you needed to hear that? This is what I'm talking about.

Throughout the book, as you're asked to emit a sound via a mantra, know that it further enhances your vibration and helps you develop your ability to use your free will.

FREE WILL

This is where things get interesting. Your free will is all about choice. To choose means to invite. If I choose to focus on Spirit (light, love), I am inviting Spirit in. If I choose to focus on fear (doubt, lack), I am inviting ego in. You get to choose whether your emotions are a resource for expanding your energy, consciousness, and higher abilities, or a roadblock to connecting to your higher self or others. The choice is up to you.

Yet because most of us were taught to label our emotions as good, bad, better, or worse, it makes sense that you may have unintentionally made choices that did more harm than good. For example, if you tell yourself you could get hurt and to be careful of dating the wrong kind of person, then this naturally will cause you to close yourself off a bit as a form of protection. The challenge is that, without awareness, you might also shut down your intuitive abilities in the process. At some point you must decide what's more important: protecting yourself from getting hurt, or strengthening your connection to Spirit.

The cool part is that in the process you'll notice how activating your higher knowing is the best form of protection. Think of free will as free flow of energy. When you recite a mantra such as *Ram* or *Om*, you are consciously choosing to cultivate a current of energy. Once the energy is generated, you'll observe how it activates Spirit, intuitive abilities in the next step for Cleanse, covered in the next chapter.

Another example of interrupted or misdirected free will is when you have trouble getting started on something you chose. For example, maybe you purchased a gym membership but rarely attend, or you signed up for a class and are having a hard time completing assignments. You made the initial move (followed your gut) yet can't quite get yourself into the groove. This is likely because you have emotions looking to be processed. Without emotions in flow, you may inadvertently create space for self-doubt and insecurity to set in. Cleansing can help.

When I asked my higher guides about this, they described the process as relearning. For example, if you're used to writing with your right hand and then suddenly put the pen in your left hand, it feels awkward and uncomfortable. You may even think to yourself, *I can't do it.* Yet, with patience and practice, you could probably teach yourself how to write with your left hand. The same goes for learning how to use your free will. At first you may use it to make the initial choice, listen to your gut and sign up for the class, but then somewhere along the line you shut down your free will abilities and rather than feel your emotions as you move through the course, you start to manage what you feel. Here's the challenge: the more you cope with or manage a situation, the less you feel, and soon your ability to use your free will wisely is lost.

The Cleanse process will help you sustain states of feeling long enough so that your intuitive abilities begin to override your thinking. Like my guides mentioned with the left-hand example, it does take time and practice. To keep you on board, remember this: feeling brings you back to states of love; overthinking moves you away from it.

According to the Hermetic teachings, which combine ancient Greek and Egyptian thought, humans can be both free *and* bound. *The Kybalion: A Study of the Hermetic Philosophy of Ancient Egypt and Greece* tells us: "The further the creation is from the Centre, the more it is bound; the nearer the Centre it reaches, the nearer Free is it." One could interpret this many ways. But I've asked my Spirit guides about this, and the answer I receive is "love." Love is the center of creation. The further you move away from love (this includes loving yourself, by the way), the less free will you have.

> Love is the center of creation. The further you move away from love (this includes loving yourself, by the way), the less free will you have.

Therefore, you have to ask yourself, when you say things like "I need a new job," is there a part of you that is judging the job you have? And if so, isn't this a sign that you are moving away from the center (love)? Follow this rule: always move toward—not away from—love. These are the qualities closer to Source energy. This is where your higher self and spiritual team reside.

I'll give another example. A client once asked me to ask Spirit about his career because he was getting ready to attend college and wasn't sure what direction to go in. When I asked Spirit, I saw in my mind's eye a shepherd herding many sheep, then I saw an image of a large dog. I said to my client, "Have you ever wanted to work with animals?"

He replied, "Yes, I wanted to be a veterinarian, but my uncle is one, and he pretty much killed that dream."

"What do you mean?" I asked.

"He just told me not to do it."

"Yes, but you have healing hands, you may do it differently than him. You may energetically and medically help animals heal."

Hearing things put this way was all it took for this young man to follow the energy of his heart, remove all self-imposed restrictions, and give himself permission to connect to and co-create by tuning into the things he loved, like animals.

It's perfectly fine to get other people's opinions, yet when their comments or remarks come in the form of fear, bitterness, or judgment, you can pretty much guess this information is not coming from their higher selves. I remember when I started writing my first book, I called some local authors to get their advice. One told me not to go with traditional publishing houses because they put her book out of print, while another told me it's impossible to get picked up by traditional publishers. I could sense the frustration in their comments and from that point forward decided not to consult with anyone on book writing who didn't show evidence of success.

Otherwise, without realizing it, you may internalize their beliefs, experiences, and happenings as if they were your own. Please, don't use your free will in this way. Don't accept something as truth if it has zero to little feeling involved. Instead, use these moments as opportunities to re-center yourself. Process your emotions and turn to your higher guidance.

> Don't accept something as truth if it has zero to little feeling involved.

Here's the thing: most things that people say are based on their own internal triggers. When you ask them questions, you're giving them an opportunity to release and express their own emotions. So, if someone spews their frustrations, give them the freedom to do so (as long as it is respectful), and walk away knowing you probably helped that person in some way. Yet it doesn't mean you have to take their frustrations on as if they were your own.

Should you miss something along the way or slip back into reactivity, trust that your higher guidance is always there and will return to assist you. This is in accordance with the spiritual laws of correspondence and rhythm. In the case of the young man who wanted advice about his career, he texted me a couple of hours after our session. He opened up a letter from a college and inside the envelope was a picture of a large dog. It was the same exact breed I saw in my mind's eye. My client took this as a sign, a validation from the universe, that working with animals in some way may very well be a part of his path.

Know at any time you can call on a member of your spiritual team to assist you with your free will. Ask them to help you connect more consistently to your higher self and to help you use your free will wisely. They will help you along the way.

If you are still unsure about how to tap into your free will efficiently, saying two simple words will help: *thank you*. Each time you say thank you to the universe, your guides, or higher self, you are choosing to see the blessing in every situation, even the stuff that doesn't look or feel so great. Gratitude is a real way to raise your frequency or vibration.

Another client, who had removed all social media from her phone to help her overcome depression, came to me with some concerns. She had started a business and realized that not having any social media could potentially sabotage her growth. Although removing social media was such a bold and courageous move on her part, she now needed to learn how to have a healthy relationship with social media. I encouraged her to say thank you like this:

> Thank you for giving me this opportunity to share my business with the world.
>
> Thank you, Spirit guides, for connecting me to the customers most interested in my product.

Your turn!

*Thank you, Spirit, for*_____

Fill in the blank with words like guidance, wisdom, love, compassion, growth.

HEART

When you say thank you to Spirit, you open your heart with love and gratitude. That's what I learned from Leanne. When she came to see me, it wasn't long before I realized many of the people around her behaved like bullies. In other words, rather than process their own emotions, they "managed" them by teasing Leanne or taking advantage of her gentle nature. After moving through a few Cleanses with Leanne and asking Spirit, the message I received was that Leanne needed to understand the difference between responding from her head versus her heart.

While it may seem like being nice, mellow, or respectful comes from the heart, Spirit did not present it that way (at least not in this case). Instead, Spirit suggested her niceness created a wishy-washy, flip-floppy kind of energy. When I said to Leanne, "Spirit keeps saying the words 'wishy-washy' to me. What does that mean?" Leanne responded, "That is me! I am flip-floppy. I can never commit or make a decision."

That day, through Cleansing and asking Spirit, Leanne and I learned how wishy-washy energy can make it easy for others to take advantage of her by causing her to not really take a stance. Leanne was associating her wishy-washiness with freedom. She believed if she didn't commit fully to something (for example, a decision, a relationship), she was free. Yet Spirit told me otherwise.

Your heart doesn't just help you purify energy and transform fear, it also stabilizes you. Think of something or someone you love right now. If that person (maybe your child or sibling) made a terrible mistake, would you still love them? You might not approve of what they did or said, yet your heart is still strong. Spiritual beings teach us about the importance of being connected to our hearts. Archangel Sophia is one of them. She is the angel of truth and wisdom, and when called upon she will help you connect to your true self. She is one of the guides (along with Archangel Michael) who taught me the value of emanating my true self (love) into my *bio-field*.

BIO-FIELD

If I asked you how the Internet works, and you told me to go into the settings on my computer and connect it to Wi-Fi using a password, it would give me enough information to make a connection, but still no understanding of how it works. Yet, if I asked you how the Internet works and you explained how all data sent over the Internet is translated into pulses of light or electricity, also called *bits*, and then interpreted by the receiving computer, this might give me a better sense of how it all *really* happens. It's the same with asking Spirit.

According to the Institute of Biodynamic Medicine Ltd.,

> The "bio-field" is the electromagnetic field [EMF] within and surrounding living organisms. The "aura" is the name given to the emanations of bioenergy when measured by Kirlian photography, but it can be measured in other ways as well, like gas discharge visualization, biophoton emission, laser therapy, infrared thermography, static magnetic fields, pulsed EMF therapies, EMF-light, electrical current, vibration, and sound. Any of these measurement tools is looking to quantify what emanates from energy centers in the body, along, out, and beyond the "exits" (head, hands, and feet) and through the skin—when we are relaxed and free from stress.

Here is the interesting part: "As bioenergy is freed within a person, we can have a feeling of 'waking up' and becoming more 'alive.' We 'come to our senses,' including the sixth sense of intuition."

❀

Right now, you may have learned to call upon your spiritual team by verbalizing out loud or to yourself things like *I call upon my spiritual guides, I call upon my spiritual team, for protection*. And if that is the case, I encourage you to keep asking and inviting your guides in to be a part of your life. I also encourage you to take it a step further, by noticing what happens after you *hum* or recite another mantra out loud in step three. Give it a try right now.

Sit up tall, take a nice, long, deep inhale through your nose, inflating your lower abdomen.

On the exhale, *hum* out loud as you pull your navel toward your spine one time.

Pause and notice what you feel.

It's likely you noticed an increase of sensations, and if you really pay attention, it can feel like ripples of water expanding outward, like rings in a pond after you throw a pebble into the water.

Notice how the *hum* expands into your bio-field. Like the Internet collecting "bits" of information, only instead of data you receive things like sensations, changes in temperature, tingles, goose bumps, colors, images, sounds (music or words), epiphanies *(aha!)*, or pure energy (presence or inner knowing).

As you expand outward into your aura (energetically), this impacts energy centers closer to your physical body in a positive way. These energy centers are called *chakras*.

CHAKRAS

The word *chakra* means "wheel or cycle of energy." There are seven main chakras or energy centers situated along the spine. Think of chakras as being like sails on an old-fashioned windmill. When they are in balance, they spin clockwise at a smooth, rhythmic rate. When your chakras are out of balance, the energy that pools there becomes slow, sluggish, backward, or blocked. When energy is not moving freely, this can negatively impact both your mental and physical health leading to, for example, tension and stress.

By using a pendulum (a tool that detects the movement of invisible energy) and/or muscle testing, I have tested hundreds of clients before and after Cleansing. I've been able to see how the mindful practices in Cleanse can help bring energy into balance. Yet working with energy is a tricky thing. It likes to revert back to old habits and patterns, and this is why practices such as conscious breathing and chanting to move energy need to be done consistently. Some channelers and psychics can see chakras, yet for most they are invisible to the human eye. Many spiritual teachers, including Caroline Myss, PhD, refer to these energy centers as the anatomy of Spirit. In fact, one of Dr. Myss's books is titled *Anatomy of the Spirit*.

Once your chakras are in balance, one thing you may notice is that the way you tune into Spirit may shift. For example, if your eyes are looking upward, this may mean that you are constructing your thoughts or forming a mental picture in your mind: visual processing. According to neurolinguistic programming (NLP), certain eye movements and direction can indicate thinking, that is, using the analytical mind. Yet when you are connecting to Spirit, you may find your gaze shifts to looking steadily along the horizon, side to side, or that you are closing your eyes to move inward. Most energy workers (including myself) either close their eyes when they receive messages, or have a steady, trancelike, or neutral gaze. Another way to recognize if you are connected to Spirit or in a state of processing your emotions (which often is experienced after a Cleanse) is if you feel an overall sense of oneness or ease.

Scientists at Yale University offered a little bit more insight as to why this occurs when they studied activity in the *parietal cortex* of the brain. This area of the brain involves awareness of self and others as well as attention processing. According to a study published on-line in the journal *Cerebral Cortex,* "Spiritual experiences can be re-ligious in nature or not, such as a feeling of oneness when you are in nature" (Lisa Miller). Whether you are in nature, Cleansing, or sitting on the couch of your living room, you'll see how you are able to connect with this state of oneness. You'll know because you'll find yourself more tuned into the here and now. In this state, your atten-tion is becoming more refined, and you will be more apt to pick up on little clues, signs, messages, and vibrations of Spirit.

ATTENTION

You'll likely find (as I do) that it's common to go back and forth between the analytical mind and connecting with Spirit. It can feel much like a dropped signal when you're talking on a cell phone. Should this occur, a gentle and effective way to reconnect is to recite a mantra, such as *aad* or *hum. Hum* out loud for about five seconds. As you get to know your spiritual team you'll begin to notice when they're around you and when you no longer sense your connec-tion. I often feel my spirit guides—archangels and ascended beings, which are high vibrational beings of love and light—in the same way I might experience a team huddle. The energy feels supportive, protective, and loving. Should you get distracted (and who the heck doesn't these days?) and your attention waver, set an intention to connect to your spiritual team either by humming out loud or visu-alizing the infinity sign above your head. This ought to do the trick.

I'll introduce you to your spiritual team in the next chapter. Let's take a moment right now to call them in and practice that *hum* mantra right now.

CLEANSE HIGHLIGHT: *E,* EMIT

The purpose of step three is to continue to increase the vibration in your body and connection to Spirit through the production of sound. Sound creates a vibratory channel between you
and Spirit. When you produce sound by reciting a mantra, many
things happen; one is you learn how to exercise your free will,
and another is you release attachments (ego).

In Part 3, you will have the opportunity to practice several
different mantras. Right now, take a moment to practice the *hum.*
It can help to know the meaning of what you are repeating. In
Sanskrit, *hum* is the mantra of enlightenment. Please note humming itself has many mental and physical health benefits from
increasing blood flow, improving circulation, and releasing stress
to toning your vagus nerve and moving you out of fight or flight
into calm and ease.

When you *hum,* be sure to sit up tall and bring your chin
parallel to the earth. On the inhale, inflate your lower abdomen
like a balloon, and on the exhale, recite *hum.* After humming,
observe how the energy flows in and out (like the ocean tide)
into your aura, cleansing (like the way the ocean tide cleans the
shores) along the way. Learning how to observe from the space
of inner stillness is key to learning how to effectively use your
free will.

CHAPTER 4

YOUR SPIRITUAL TEAM

There is only one emotion: love.
Everything else is a reaction.

Anna has been my personal psychic medium for at least a decade. I visit her one or two times a year or when I have a major decision to make. As I wrote this book, Anna was eighty-eight years old. What I love about her is that she has a strong faith and a lot of life experience. In her younger years she worked as a psychic with detectives. In many ways she has been a bit of an earth angel for me. When my marriage was in the worst possible shape ever, she was the one who encouraged me to fight for what was important to me. And some of my favorite memories are the times we sat at her kitchen table while she taught me things like how to read the tarot deck and figure out someone's life-path number (which helps you identify your life-path mission) through numerology. When I sit down with her, she always reminds me, "You are a five, the teacher."

Sometimes the readings Anna gave me really helped while other times they seemed vague. Like the time when she pulled the tarot cards, placed them in a certain arrangement on the table, put her finger on one card, and said, "This one represents your mother-in-law, and she is not well." This was not really a surprise to me as my mother-in-law has the worse diet on the planet and at that time was nearly eighty-seven. She also can be quite the handful, but I won't get into that here.

I was hoping to get to the good stuff. Maybe after all these years Anna would tell me things I really wanted to hear, like "Your book will hit the *New York Times* bestseller list, your children are happy and healthy, and, oh yeah, Oprah is gonna call you."

Yet this was not the case. Instead, I heard things like "You have to be more confident, believe in yourself, be careful people don't take advantage of you, they will steal your ideas, leave you in the dust, and your husband is very stressed about work." *Augh.*

"You're very smart, Sherianna," she said. "Look what you have created! It is just that you are too nice sometimes."

"Thank you," I replied, gave her fifty dollars in cash, and left.

Has this ever happened to you? Perhaps you left a reading feeling a little disappointed or deflated? Yet something inside me told me Anna was right—it was time for me to quit wavering, be more confident. At the time, I had no idea all this would happen naturally the more familiar I became with my spiritual team.

WHAT IS A SPIRITUAL TEAM?

I've mentioned them already, but let's dive in! Your spiritual team can include anyone or anything with a soul, from a loved one who has passed, such as a grandmother or a former pet, to the soul of a tree you once had in your front yard. Some spirit guides have lived many lives, such as ascended beings like Buddha and Jesus, or are personal guides, such as an indigenous shaman. Some people use the words "spiritual team" and "spiritual guides" interchangeably while others use the term "spirit guides."

Your team may also include spirit animals or other types of Nature spirits, fairies, and high celestial beings of pure love and light, such as archangels and guardian angels. Your spirit guides know who the members of your spiritual team are, and will often communicate with them on your behalf when you ask for support, guidance, healing, and more.

Think of your spiritual team as you might have gotten to know your classmates in school—it takes time. With some people it may feel awkward or distant while other relationships may happen more naturally and easily. Try your best not to judge the experience. Instead, choose to connect to your higher self. When you are connected to your higher self, this helps you feel very much a part of the team (class) as opposed to an outsider. This is why in Part 3 I encourage you to always connect with your higher self first, and if you forget, the steps of the Cleanse can help.

Without this "team spirit," you may feel like you're on the outside looking inward. Trust that when you are connected to your higher self, you are connected to your Spirit. One way to tell is you feel very much a part of what is happening in that moment. You don't just look at a picture of Archangel Michael carrying a sword; you're able to ask questions about his sword, what exactly it is used for, and how it may help you in your spiritual journey. I've asked these kinds of questions to many of my clients, each time getting valuable insights about their own journeys, Source, energy, healing, and more. When you are connected, you sense energy, vibration, oneness, love, and more. Therefore, when you think of your spiritual team, I want to be sure you always include yourself.

With that said, I'm not sure if it's possible for your human brain to capture the enormity of your team. While there is so much happening in the spiritual realms, your guides don't come from ego. Therefore, they don't compete or try to outdo one another. Instead, when you ask, they work in harmony, stepping in and out as needed. This is their way of providing space for other spiritual guides to come in who may be better equipped to support you. Think of it as an honor when you see, sense, or notice a new powerful presence. This could very well be a sign you've mastered some of the lessons you came here to learn and are now ready for new ones.

One way you can both connect to your higher self and the other team members is to tune into the *Rays of Light*.

THE RAYS OF LIGHT

The Rays of Light are high vibrational frequencies that are referred to in several religions and esoteric philosophies including Gnosticism, Mithraism, Catholicism, and Hinduism. They are guided by ascended masters and archangels. When you see and sense the presence of a Ray of Light, you can pretty much bet you are connected to your higher self and spiritual team. When I was trained as a quantum healer, I learned how to work with the Rays of Light to help balance someone's energetic field (aura) and chakras. Since then, my guides have given me more input on the Rays of Light, indicating that they exist within us and are in fact part of our soul makeup. So trust that these Rays of Light are part of your makeup. In other words, as you clear your energy, detox reactions, and give yourself permission to feel, your vibration increases. As this occurs, higher frequencies (your inner Rays of Light) can shine through.

As Alice Bailey points out, "The seven senses are, in a peculiar way, the physical plane correspondences of the seven rays, and are closely related to and governed by them all" (*Esoteric Psychology 1*, p. 133).

The Rays of Light reveal themselves in a variety of colors such as violets, yellows, and shades of white. Many people see these Rays of Light when they meditate, and some of my students have captured them on camera in ways that unmistakably look like angels. Similar to auras and chakras, their colors can change moment to moment, breath by breath. How the Rays of Light differ from what we think of visually as colors is that these rays cannot be measured. For example, the color red has a wavelength of 620–750 nanometers (nm) and a frequency of 400–484 hertz (Hz). The Rays of Light emanate from Source, Creator, or God and therefore are considered to be infinite in nature (just like us). Each ray of light carries godlike frequencies such as pure peace and freedom. Because you come from Source you also carry these qualities. Connecting to the Rays of Light through the development of your senses helps you align with the godlike forces; as Alice Bailey states, "The soul, through the medium of the brain, causes revelations. It throws light into the brain, and thus the way of human beings becomes increasingly illumined" (p. 132). It is not uncommon for individuals to "see" (through their mind's eye), sense, or feel the Rays of Light during a Cleanse.

After over a decade of working as an energy healer, I have had the privilege of witnessing the magic of these rays, how they bring peace and harmony to clients. If a client can't sense the light or if it's weak, then I know they could benefit from taking part in additional Chakra Cleanses such as the ones provided in Part 3. The key is to remember that just because you don't "see" the Rays of Light in your mind's eye, it doesn't mean they're not there. I had one client who was taking part in a group I was offering who was so frustrated because everyone else was reporting their experiences with the light and she just couldn't get there. I reminded her that just because she couldn't sense it doesn't mean she wasn't receiving it. Then as if by magic this started to change, and she became quite equipped at connecting to the rays. What I've found is your connection to Spirit can be impacted by the level of traumas in your life. My recommendation is to be patient and compassionate with yourself along the way.

VIBRATIONAL FREQUENCIES	
Here is a little bit more information about the Rays of Light and the vibrational frequencies; each one harnesses vibrational qualities such as:	
White Purification	New beginnings, peace
Gold	Frequencies of protection, Christ consciousness, unconditional love
Silver	Divine Mother and universal consciousness frequency, balance
Diamond	Great for clearing generational complications
Violet	Ray of transmutation, forgiveness, alchemy
Purple	Wonderful for grounding in love, transformation
Blue	Protection, faith, trust, true power
Magenta	Cosmic transformation, unity, peace, cosmic divine love
Green	Healing, abundance, truth
Orange	Deep soul and subconscious healing
Pink	Divine love, patience
Peach	Enlightenment
Aqua and White	Holy Spirit
Yellow	Inner strength, resilience, manifesting
Red	Grounding in God's love, transformation

While I was writing this book, I saw the flyer for a mediumship circle that piqued my interest. I decided to give it a whirl as "field research." The instructor, Rick, was one of the kindest, most humble teachers I have ever met, with a rich understanding of spirituality. Then one evening, a spirit came to me during one of our class meditations. It was a man who looked to be about forty years of age. I could see him clear as day. The overall sense I got was that he had a rough life and had gotten himself in quite a bit of trouble with the law. During my meditation, I asked silently if he had a message he wanted me to deliver, and his response was "No, no one wants to hear from me." Although I had compassion for this man in spirit, I knew he was not part of my spiritual team. Not just because I didn't recognize him, but because I've become so familiar with the energy of my team.

Just as you may feel the difference between the energy of a loved one or a stranger, you'll also get better at distinguishing different energies as you work with Spirit. For example, you'll develop the ability to discern the difference between the energy of an ascended being (also referred to as ascended masters or lords of the rays) and a loved one (like a grandfather who has passed) in Spirit.

ASCENDED BEINGS

Ascended beings are considered enlightened individuals who once walked the earth. Because they've lived many lives, they've progressed through a series of lessons, rebirths, and challenges. They've made positive choices and as a result have gone through higher and higher spiritual transformations. Through various incarnations, ascended beings have risen beyond the physical realm. They exist on higher planes of consciousness and have chosen to devote their existence to helping humans. They are the great healers, leaders, or prophets who have evolved to higher levels of being within the spiritual hierarchy. Some examples are Jesus, Buddha, Mother Mary, or the Blessed Mother, Krishna, Confucius, and the saints.

Think of getting to know your spiritual team the way you may have first learned to identify emotions by name (maybe anger, sadness), facial expressions (a grimace versus a smile), bodily responses (stomping feet, walking fast), or sensations (feeling hot, tense, calm, cool). And instead of emotions it will be archangels and angels (which often feel light and sometimes tingly), ascended beings (stabilizing, calming, grounding, and full of love), and Spirit guides (supportive and present). I don't know about you, but I find it interesting that emotions in a processing, flow state and Spirit can feel similar in the body. For example, the emotions of joy and happiness feel much like the energy of an archangel to me while feelings of confidence, strength, and protection represent the presence of an ascended being.

I also notice a pulsing sensation around my third eye—the space above and between my eyebrows—and energy running up and down my legs when an ascended being is present. When archangels arrive (as they will), sometimes I find myself scratching the hair on my head, yawning, or standing still as if my feet were anchored in cement.

I also see wings and flashes of light in my mind's eye when an archangel is around. With ascended beings, for whatever reason, I have an easier time hearing (remember clairaudience) their messages, whereas I am better at feeling (clairsentience) messages from archangels. When I go to sleep at night, my dreams are filled with Spirits, guides so vivid I can make out their faces and personality.

ASCENDED BEINGS CAN HELP US . . .
Gain knowledge and wisdom.
Awaken true power and abilities.
Shift consciousness both individually and globally.
Cultivate peace and harmony.
Align and activate with light.
Align with your Creator, oneness, or God.
Receive divine protection.
Transmute and transform old emotional patterns, and cycles of reactivity.
Prepare for ascension.
Resolve karma.
Heal.

SOME OF THE ASCENDED BEINGS MOST OFTEN ASSOCIATED WITH THE RAYS OF LIGHT	
Gold	Ascended being Jesus (also known as the Christ consciousness frequency)
White	Buddha
Diamond	Ma ha Cohan
Magenta	Mary Magdalene
Blue	Lord Lanto, El Morya, Mother Mary
Yellow	Kuthumi, I have experienced Mother Mary with this ray as well.
Ruby Red	Lady Nadia
Violet	St. Germaine
Purple	Merlin
Silver/Pale Blue	Divine Mother Consciousness, Mother Mary
Pink	Paul the Venetian
Green	Master Hilarion (formally Paul the Apostle)
Orange	Ganesh

Remember the ascended beings with their numerous incarnations have likely been where you are in life. So, for example, if you are having a tough time co-parenting with your ex, and worried about the impact this might be having on your children, you might want to call on the Mother Mary or Mary Magdalene to assist you. They understand your situation and will help you . . . when you ask.

ARCHANGELS

Let's say you're going to court over a situation and feel like the other person is not telling the truth. You may want to call on a specific archangel such as Archangel Sophia, who is wonderful at helping you get to the truth or the heart of the matter. Archangels are another integral element of our spiritual team.

Archangels and angels are messengers of God. The English word *angel* comes from the Greek word *angelos*, which means "to send." The word *arch* symbolizes their higher position as chief messengers of God. Both words *angels* and *archangel* end in the suffix *el*, which means God. The *iel* at the end of most archangel names (for example, Gabriel or Uriel) means "of God" or "strength of God." (By the way, although we tend to think of Archangel Michael as male, and Archangel Jophiel as female, for example, *iel* is a gender-neutral merging of the masculine and feminine. Because they are pure spirit, angels and archangels have no gender as we understand it.) By reciting, chanting, or singing an archangel's name out loud or in a prayer or meditation, you'll be able to receive the beautiful healing and nourishing frequencies of these beings of light.

Archangels are nondenominational and offer love and support no matter what religion, nonreligious, or spiritual belief system you have. Unlike ascended beings, archangels never lived in a physical body or walked the earth. Religions including Christianity, Catholicism, Islam, Hindu, and Judaism recognize archangels. Within these religions, Michael and Gabriel seemed to be referred to the most. Their vibrational frequency can be quite soothing and calming to your body. As a result, when connecting with one of them, you may find yourself being a little bit more patient; this is likely because you're taking a moment to receive their light. As this occurs, your willingness to be open and present supersedes the urge to act or respond quickly.

I remember a client named Sue who moved through a few Cleanses with me one morning. Later that day, she turned on the television set, and the channel was on a particular movie. She started watching it and discovered that one of the characters in the film was going through her exact situation. She said to me later, "I felt like I was watching myself on television." She could relate so deeply to the character's pain she started to weep. Since Sue hardly had time to watch movies (let alone by herself with no one else in the house), she took the opportunity to let herself cry. She felt like it was the work of the archangels. For so long she had been harboring and holding back everything she felt. What were the chances that we would discuss her situation in a session, we would call in the angels, and then she would find herself watching this movie with zero distractions?

This may be how it happens for you. You may find yourself weeping for no reason at all. This is often the work of the angels sending you healing in that exact moment. This is what happens when you give permission to your spiritual team to come around you. Soon you will see how the archangels and ascended beings can give you even more support when you let go of resistance and start giving yourself permission to feel.

Here are some of the archangels you can look forward to connecting to. According to the Hearts Center, "Each of the seven rays has a presiding archangel and archeia who embody the quality of that ray and direct the angelic bands serving under them on that ray. The primary role of the archangels is to radiate celestial light into our world for the freeing and saving of souls and for the illumination and freedom of life" (heartscenter.org). Therefore, if you see colors that don't match the archangel, sometimes it means you are connecting to the divine feminine aspect (archeia). The most important part is to keep an open mind.

ARCHANGELS	
Archangel Gabriel	White
Archangel Sandalphon	Golds, blues, and ambers
Archangel Seraphiel	Amber
Archangel Raziel	Diamond
Archangel Michael	Blue
Archangel Raphael	Green and orange
Archangel Chamuel	Pink
Archangel Uriel	Violet and red
Archangel Jophiel	Yellow
Archangel Zadkiel	White, violet, and purple
Archangel Anthriel	Magenta
Archangel Mariel	Magenta
Archangel Sophia	Indigo
Archangel Metatron	Purplish blue and indigo

When an archangel is around, I often feel a tingly sensation in my hair so much that I want to scratch it. Archangels are here to assist with:

Protection

Healing (emotional, physical)

Truth

Forgiveness

Helping you fulfill your purpose

Guidance, reassurance, support

GUARDIAN ANGELS

While archangels are chief messengers of God for everyone, guardian angels are more specific to you. It's said that everyone has a least one guardian angel and they are with us from the moment we are born until death. Your guardian angel loves you unconditionally and will never abandon you. Some people are curious about who their guardian angel is, so they might ask Spirit for their name during or after a meditation. Others are more interested in feeling, sensing, and noticing when they are around. Some psychics and mediums believe that guardian angels have the ability to show up in physical form. Here are some signs your guardian angels are nearby:

- Change in the temperature (for example, coolness) in the room
- Flash of a light
- Feeling or sensing a presence
- Feeling like you are not alone (a presence behind you or by your side)
- Cloud formations in the sky
- Hearing or seeing things you can't explain
- Tingly sensation on the crown of your head or around your feet
- Seeing the same entity or receiving messages in a dream

Should you sense, receive energy, healing, or reassurance from an archangel, ascended being, or guardian angel, you can thank them by lighting a candle or incense. It brings them joy to know their love for you was fully received.

SPIRIT GUIDES

According to author Sonia Choquette, "Angels are there to walk you through your life path and help you fulfill your purpose" (Belief .net). She states that angels have never had a physical incarnation. Spirit guides have once been in physical form. She refers to Spirit guides as assistants or "helpers" (Belief.net).

Each of your guides comes with specific expertise in certain areas. I like to think of Spirit guides as coaches and teachers. I believe one of my Spirit guides was a former writer to the point to which I wonder at times who is really writing the book. Whatever it is you are going through, whether it be physical, emotional, or career challenges, there is a Spirit guide there to help you. For example, you can call on a Spirit guide to help you study for a test. These would be guides that are focused on education, communication, and learning. Something as simple as "I call upon my learning guides" can do the trick.

LOVED ONES

When thinking about or referring to their spiritual team, many people like to include loved ones who have passed. Some psychics and mediums don't consider loved ones as part of the holy community of the spiritual team while others do. As an Emotional Detox coach, I think if it helps someone to process what they feel, why not? Many people get such relief when they know their loved ones are looking to communicate with them.

Some of these loved ones may have been close to you when they were in the physical realm, and you may not have had the opportunity to meet others. Regardless, they are still your loved ones. My daughter was skateboarding at night in our neighborhood when she came home out of breath, freaking out. "Mom," she said, "I saw a Spirit, it was a little girl, she came right in front of me." When I shared this story with Mark Anthony, who calls himself the Psychic Lawyer, he asked me if I'd lost a baby. I said, "Yes, I had a miscarriage years ago." He responded, "That Spirit your daughter saw was her; she is scaring your daughter on purpose. She wants her to stop skateboarding at night. She is worried your daughter is going to get hit by a car." My daughter never skateboarded at night again. *Thank you, Spirit.*

SPIRIT GUIDES CAN BE . . .
A loved one who has passed away, even a pet
Someone you knew in this lifetime or another lifetime
Someone from another lifetime who understands your situation (maybe they went through what you're going through and want to assist you)
A soul who has the skill set to support you (for example, a shaman if you are a healer)
A guardian angel
Archangel
Ascended being
Don't forget, *you* are part of the team!

SPIRIT GUIDES CAN HELP YOU TRANSMUTE EMOTIONS, REACTIONS, AND PATTERNS INTO HIGHER STATES OF PEACE AND EASE	
Self-criticism	Self-love
Taking things personally	Resilience
Fear	Inner strength
Guilt	Compassion, confidence
Discouragement	Hope
Shame	Strength
Sadness	Healing

Call on your spiritual team using a singsong voice. Try saying something like this:

I call upon the Rays of Light, asking you to come, I call upon the Rays of Light, we are one.

Or:

I call upon Archangel Raphael, asking you to come, I call upon Archangel Raphael, we are one.

THINGS YOU CAN ASK FOR FROM YOUR SPIRITUAL TEAM
Ideas, strategies, new insights, clarity, direction
Guidance, love, support, reassurance
Healing, release, forgiveness
Energy clearings and activations

CLEANSE HIGHLIGHT: A ACTIVATE (MEDITATE)

Now that you've moved the energy of your emotions through breathing and chanting a mantra, you are ready to notice and observe energy through meditation. To meditate means to listen and observe without judgment. Through meditation you can move the energy in your chakras as well as your aura. Similar to adjusting the dial to get better reception on a radio, the A for activate is about tuning into your psychic senses. Because it is the fourth step of the Cleanse, you are likely feeling more present and relaxed, which makes this an ideal time to ask Spirit.

CHAPTER 5

BECOMING SPIRITUALLY STRONG AND HEALTHY

At some point, you must move
beyond needing clarity to developing
self-confidence.

One would think that when you're connected to Spirit only good things would happen. Your life would be in perfect harmony; you would never feel sad, angry, or fearful again. As a result, this might lead to unrealistic expectations and fantasies about how life ought to be. Yet what I've learned from my spiritual team is that they know life on earth is full of challenges and that we could benefit from their support. While human beings like to be independent and to believe we have everything under control, it's often through things like unexpected circumstances, trials, and setbacks that we realize we are not. The important thing to remember is just because you may not have full control doesn't mean you are powerless.

In fact, asking and turning to Spirit can be one of the most powerful choices you can make. Don't just take my word for it; there's lots of research out there of how "spirituality can help address issues such as poor self-esteem, low confidence, lack of self-control, and fear of daily tasks and challenges" (McClean Hospital). In this chapter, I cover four qualities that help you become spiritually strong and healthy. After each one, I ask you to take a deeper dive through reflective questions and journaling into getting to know yourself. Remember, this is not just a journey of asking and connecting to your guides; it is also about discovering your purpose. Here are the four areas we will cover: boundaries, effective communication, forgiveness, and self-love and compassion.

Before getting there, let's look at some guidelines put out by McLean Hospital for what constitutes spiritual health.

SPIRITUAL HEALTH GUIDELINES

- Reserved and thoughtful emotional reactions—even to life's great challenges
- A healthy ability to feel and express emotions when called for, especially when dealing with grief or loss
- Daily practices to help process hardships, changes, and emotions
- An ability to deal with the challenges posed by other people with kindness and understanding

- Flexible beliefs that can adjust as needed to new circumstances or information
- Mindfulness and presence when eating, exercising, working, and enjoying time with loved ones
- The ability to explain one's inner state to others if necessary or desired

Keeping these guidelines in mind, let's look at those four main areas of spiritual strength, beginning with the ability to set boundaries.

BOUNDARIES

Boundaries are not necessarily about keeping people out but more so a way to take care of your energy. Without boundaries, your energy can become easily depleted, making it less likely you will choose to process your emotions and/or connect to your guides.

Take a moment to reflect on the following boundary-setting areas as a way for you to become spiritually strong and healthy.

Physical Boundaries

A physical boundary is related to anything physical. It can be anything from the amount of physical time you spend scrolling on your phone to creating a space in your schedule to do the things that matter (such as exercise), or creating a space in your home for meditation (or Cleansing) that is free from physical clutter.

In what areas of your life could you benefit from physical boundaries?

_____

_____

_____

_____

What realistic limits can you place on those physical
boundaries? For example, you may set a boundary that you
do not check your phone before a certain time in the morning.

Is there any physical clutter around you that may be impacting
the way you feel? What is a realistic goal you can set around
clearing these items? For example, you might begin by
cleaning out your car or sorting through one clothing drawer
a week.

Emotional Boundaries

An emotional boundary is a way to hold yourself accountable for
your emotions. For example, when we blame others for our feelings,
this may be a way we cross a boundary. The opposite can also be true:
Others may make us feel responsible for what they sense. Another
breach of this boundary is when someone expects too much from
you (or maybe you place unreal expectations yourself). The more
spiritually strong and healthy you become, the less likely you will
take ownership of emotions, situations, beliefs, and expectations that
don't belong to you.

Are you taking accountability for emotional reactivity that is
not yours? How so?

_____

_____

How might listening to Spirit and the divine messages help you to not take things personally?

_____

_____

_____

Where in your life do you feel like your energy is being pulled?

_____

_____

_____

What is one question you could ask Spirit to help you in this area?

_____

_____

_____

_____

Spiritual Boundaries

Spiritual boundaries are about what is valuable and meaningful to you. Spiritual boundaries allow you to focus on things like what you are passionate about. I often believe the soul speaks through what you are drawn to. For example, you may be drawn to animals, art, music, or nature. Another example of a spiritual boundary is when someone (or even perhaps yourself) makes you feel like you are less than. Remember, you are perfect in the eyes of your creator.

What is meaningful to you in your life?

_____
_____
_____
_____

What do you value?

_____
_____
_____
_____

What are you drawn to? What brings you joy?

_____
_____
_____
_____

What activity never gets old or boring? How does doing these activities make you feel?

_____
_____
_____
_____

When there is negative energy around, how do you protect yourself? For example, do you visualize white light, or ground your energy by going outside or taking a deep breath?

_____
_____
_____
_____

EFFECTIVE COMMUNICATION

In order to be an effective communicator with others, as well as with Spirit, you'll want to get to know the difference between constructive versus critical feedback. For example, giving one-word or vague answers is not constructive. This leaves room for false interpretations and misunderstandings. The same goes for oversharing or repeating yourself. I often see this when people ask Spirit the same question over and over again.

To be effective, it's always best to be as specific as you can. If what you have to say is emotional, do your best to always talk honestly. When it comes to communicating with Spirit, remember you will never be judged for what you say.

How do you currently communicate verbally about what you feel? For example, how do you typically begin a conversation?

_____

_____

_____

_____

How do you communicate nonverbally? For example, do you make eye contact?

_____

_____

_____

_____

When you communicate with Spirit, how does it look and sound (both verbally and nonverbally). For example, do you become quiet, still? What is the tone of your voice?

_____

_____

Is it difficult for you to come up with the right words? Are you open and willing to ask Spirit for help with this? If so, what might you ask?

In what ways do you currently listen to Spirit?

How would you like others to speak to or listen to you? How might you ask Spirit for support with this?

FORGIVENESS

Before getting into forgiveness, let me ask you this: How much energy does it take for you to remain in a state of non-forgiveness? Have you ever thought about that? Forgiveness is freedom. It doesn't mean you forget or even approve of what happened; it means you are choosing to be spiritually strong and free.

In what areas of your life have you practiced forgiveness? How did that look and feel afterward?

_____

_____

Are you open and willing to ask Spirit to assist you with forgiveness now?

_____

_____

_____

_____

Dear Spirit: Please bring forth the courage to forgive myself for

_____

_____

_____

Dear Spirit: Please bring forth the courage and strength to forgive _____

_____

_____

Thank you, Spirit.

SELF-LOVE AND COMPASSION

One of the biggest ways we suppress our emotions and Spirit is to withhold love. We give love to some but not others. We love some situations but not others, and when someone hurts us, makes us feel angry or rejected, we put up imaginary walls of resistance so love can't get in or out. In this section, reflect on ways to open yourself up to love.

The areas of my life in which I am withholding love are _____and _____.

When I withhold love, it makes me feel _____
_____.

The areas I may withhold from myself are_____
and_____.

Dear Spirit, please bring forth self-love and compassion in
these areas of my life:_____,
_____ and_____.

What are some things you are grateful for?

_____

_____

_____

_____

_____

In what ways do you show love and compassion to yourself?

_____

_____

_____

_____

In what ways do you show love and compassion to others?

_____

_____

_____

_____

_____

Exercise 1. Take a moment to sit up tall in a comfortable,
seated position away from all distractions. Close your eyes
and imagine a white infinity sign (figure eight) above your
head. Notice if it stimulates energy in your crown chakra.

Your crown chakra is known as a high spiritual energy center (often depicted as violet or white), which gives you a sense of divinity and awareness. What happens? Jot down a few thoughts:

_____

_____

_____

_____

_____

Exercise 2. Sit in a comfortable seated position away from all distractions. Relax, starting with your face, then work down to your shoulders, arms, and the rest of your body. Take one deep breath in and one out through your nose (inflating your abdomen on inhale and gently pulling your navel toward your spine on exhale). Imagine a beautiful golden light around the crown of your head. Visualize this golden light expanding outward with every breath you take. Imagine it spread throughout your whole body and aura. Do this for a few minutes and then jot down what you experienced.

_____

_____

_____

_____

_____

Now that you have taken part in exercises that help you build spiritual strength and health, take a moment to review the next step of the Cleanse: *N*, for nourish, before you move onto the next chapter.

CLEANSE HIGHLIGHT: *N,* NOURISH

In this step you will begin to *allow* and receive (channel) the wisdom, healing, and nourishment from Spirit. You will learn the modalities for channeling in Part 2.

CHAPTER 6

WHAT GETS IN THE WAY

Reactivity will always pull us apart;
emotions will bring us back together.

I was about to get online to lead a Cleanse in my virtual membership when I received a text from a client named Maria. "Can you talk?"

"Sure," I replied. "Give me five minutes." I must admit I was a little nervous. "Hi, are you okay?" I asked.

"Yes," she replied. "Everything is fine, Sherianna. I just don't know what to do with all these signs I am getting from Spirit."

Now with a smile on my face, I asked, "What signs?"

"White feathers and dimes . . . I am finding them everywhere. Here is the weird part: I have traveled through three different states for work and keep getting the same signs, they are literally following me. What do I do?"

"Did you google the spiritual meaning of a white feather?"

"Yup," she said.

"Then your next step is to write these little signs in your notebook and be sure to record how it made you feel when it caught your attention. How did these signs make you feel, by the way?"

"Shocked. Surprised."

"Were you able to fully process those feelings?"

"I'm not sure; how do I know if I did or did not?"

In that moment, I felt the energy around my abdomen tighten; the feeling you might get when you're digesting food and you get a little uncomfortable.

This is quite common when receiving messages from Spirit. Sometimes the information moves through you in a way in which you might experience the physical sensations of another for a moment. If the discomfort continues after a minute or turns into pain, then it might be something you need to pay attention to and even contact your doctor about. Yet, if it hangs out in the discomfort area, meaning it is tolerable and shows up for no longer than one minute, it could be either Spirit giving you a clue or your intuitive senses are reading the energy of another. Yet, if you panic, think it is your energy, and have zero knowledge about any of this, it sure could interfere with your ability to connect.

"What is getting in the way of you fully receiving the messages?"

When it came to my client Maria, who was seeing the white feathers but unsure if she had processed her emotions, Spirit guided me to ask: "What is getting in the way of you fully receiving the messages?"

In what seemed like a nanosecond, Maria blurted out, "Unworthiness." As soon as she said it a flash of orange (the color most associated with second chakra) popped into my mind's eye. Your second chakra energy center has to do with things like relationships and family history. When it's out of balance you may experience low confidence or find yourself revisiting old ways of managing emotions. I then guided Maria through the Chakra Cleanse for the second chakra like the one you will find in Part 3.

Immediately after moving through the Cleanse, I sensed a shift in Maria's energy. She felt calm, open, and centered. I then asked her to reimagine finding the white feathers and dimes as she closed her eyes. "Only this time," I said, "see yourself really taking in the energy of those messages." It was then that Maria could fully receive the offerings with a sense of calm and really take in the reassurance, blessings, offerings, and divine protection Spirit was offering.

What gets in the way of you connecting with Spirit? Well, there can be a number of things. For one, a lack of skills or previous experiences, and also high levels of stress, distractibility, clutter, attachments (physical and energetic), energetic imbalances, physical and mental clutter, and spiritual bypassing. I explore each one of these misconnections. Let's begin with high levels of stress.

HIGH LEVELS OF STRESS

Not all stress is bad. In fact, you need some stress to get you up and going in the morning. Without deadlines and the demands of daily living—the need for food and connection, and to pay your bills—heck, you may never get out of bed. This is not the kind of stress that interferes with your Spirit connection. It's when your stress levels become high and/or chronic that this can create wear and tear on your nervous system, making it difficult to both communicate with and interpret signals from Spirit.

Chronic stress not only numbs your emotions and contributes to this autopilot style of living; it also can make you feel overwhelmed, stuck, and trapped. Rather than feel connected to Spirit, you might ask yourself: *Where the heck is Spirit?*

It won't be until you get yourself off the treadmill of mental anguish and chatter, and quit trying to manage everything that comes your way, that you may be able to receive the lessons and learnings for your spiritual journey.

That's what happened with my client Mia, who wanted to be an actor more than anything in the world. When an opportunity to do a one-week internship for a film production company came her way, she grabbed it, even though it landed on the same week as her final exams. When she arrived, the company had her perform tasks like do a Google search on restaurants in the area as a potential location for filming. Now, behind closed doors in front of a computer, away from other types of production and with final exams on her mind, Mia was doubting her decision. Was it worth it to take this internship at this time?

By the time Mia landed on a session with me on Zoom, she was in high levels of stress. She talked nonstop about how awful the internship was and how it took so much time and energy away from her. Within the spaces of rehashing the experience, there were moments when she questioned the pathway to being an actor, was this industry really for her, and maybe this was all a sign it wasn't meant to be. Mia's high levels of stress had completely disconnected her from what once motivated and inspired her: her Spirit.

Mia and I did some extra breathwork in that session along with a couple of Chakra Cleanses to reboot her system. In many ways, I felt as if we were resuscitating her life-force energy. Once Mia felt a bit calmer and more relaxed, the lessons and learnings from that experience started to kick in. The first lesson was that she had put the film industry on a pedestal. She imagined the internship to both look and feel differently. This happens with creative people. Their imaginations can get the best of them in positive and negative ways. Since your imagination is supported by a balanced third-eye chakra, I knew the Chakra Cleanse for the sixth chakra would be an important one for Mia to move through.

Mia also learned to ask more questions to gain clarity before getting herself into these types of situations. She learned to take some time to assess the energy, maybe check out the environment or options before saying yes. She also learned to put her energy first. I suggested to Mia, as I suggest to you, to pay attention to what might be overly consuming you—things like problems, relationships, work, projects, or plans. If you can't walk away, take a break, or press pause, you are likely to miss spiritual guidance. Listen, I get it! I can get quite obsessed with writing books. Yet if I don't set boundaries, press pause, take a moment to connect with family and loved ones, I'll miss the important feedback, insights, and guidance Spirit provides.

Spirit knows what you care about, how your soul speaks, and the way these experiences will (and they will) serve your journey. But when you become overly stressed, this causes you to become less observant and more reactive to the world around you.

It's a slippery slope yet one to pay attention to. It may appear as if you are focused on something else, like your job, yet if you have become overly consumed with what you are trying to do or accomplish, this will only increase the chances you will become preoccupied by your own insecurities, fears, and perceived obstacles. When you are inattentive, your world feels smaller, packed with things to do, and things like other people's behaviors become magnified. The bottom line is distractibility impedes Spirit.

DISTRACTIBILITY

A student once reported that during her meditation she saw her guides with her alongside a beautiful river. They were helping her release her fears and traumatic experiences of the past into sacred waters. When I asked her how that made her feel, she replied, "Loved and supported." Then the next thing she said was "I really need to work on letting go." I find this to be quite common with my clients. One minute they are in a state of bliss, and within seconds, their mind wanders to other things, like what they need to improve or get better at.

If you've ever gone to a yoga class, felt calm and relaxed, then got into your car, glanced at your cell phone messages, and reverted to your old ways of reacting, you know what I mean. It's not bad or wrong when this happens but rather little signs that your mind could benefit from some additional training and discipline in attending to the present moment. You see, in order to ask Spirit, you want to be able to hold the space of high consciousness for longer periods of time. This is where group work and community can be key. You learn how to be in this space of higher consciousness, a higher vibration, for longer periods of time.

It's similar to the way your brain develops working memory. When taking notes in class, you look up at the board or PowerPoint presentation and listen to the teacher, then hold these thoughts in your brain long enough so you can write them down in your notebook or type them into your laptop. If you have a weak memory, you may have to keep looking up and down at the board to remember what it said. If the instructor changes the slide, you may find yourself getting distracted or losing important pieces of information. This is how it can feel when you interact with Spirit.

The good news is that mindful practices such as meditation can help. In fact, a study reported in the January 21, 2011, *Harvard Gazette* titled "Eight Weeks to a Better Brain" noted that: "Participants in an eight-week mindfulness meditation program appear to make measurable changes in brain regions associated with memory, sense of self, empathy, and stress . . . a team led by Harvard-affiliated researchers at Massachusetts General Hospital reported the results of their study, the first to document meditation-produced changes over time in the brain's gray matter."

When it comes to asking Spirit, you are building the memory of recalling words, information, and images that you witness in these high-consciousness states so you can transition into translating and delivering these messages onto paper (your journal) with more ease. One additional tip I learned indirectly from my eighty-eightish-year-old psychic friend is to put my finger on top of a word (this helps you focus and concentrate), the name of a person, or a question. For example, say I was delivering a message from Spirit for you. I would move into a state of feeling via the Cleanse method and then ask you what question you had for Spirit. I then write down the question verbatim. Then to hold my energy, I take my pointer finger and rub it back and forth over the question on the piece of paper (again to help me stay focused and connected to the energy). Using the sense of touch helps me hold my attention on the question I'm asking on your behalf; otherwise, my mind might wander.

I've also used this technique when communicating with an arch-angel, ascended being, or ray of light. For example, when I run my Membership group, I write the name of the ray of light (let's say it's the silver ray), rub my finger over it, and deliver a message to the group. Or you might write Archangel Michael and rub your finger across the name a few times as a way to train yourself to hold your focus long enough to receive a message from him.

Another trick I've learned is that when the energy feels weak, meaning I am having trouble connecting, it may be because I am dehydrated, or my body feels dysregulated. For example, if the room is too hot or cold, or I can hear noise around me, or notifications are going off on my phone, this can cause me to feel distracted. There-fore, before you journal or color (explained in Parts 2 and 3), it can be a good practice to have a bottle of water or cup of tea, move to a quiet spot, turn off your phone notifications, and make yourself comfortable (fuzzy socks or blanket, anyone?). But be sure to sit up tall when you connect so your spine is long; this makes it easier to take deep breaths. These little habits can make a significant differ-ence in your *Just Ask Spirit* practice, along with making sure your environment is free from excessive clutter.

CLUTTER

I always say what's happening on the outside of you is often a re-flection of what is happening on the inside. When our environments lose their structure or become cluttered with stuff, this can often be an early warning sign of the development of inner chaos or over-whelm. Without awareness, breath, and Spirit, it can be so easy to walk by the pile of papers or become desensitized to the pile of dirty laundry in the corner.

"Clutter reflects an overabundance of possessions that collectively create chaotic and disorderly living spaces," DePaul University psychology professor Joseph Ferrari, PhD, told *Everyday Health*. "Clutter is often the result of an overattachment to our personal items, which makes it difficult to part with them. It isn't abundance that's the problem as much as attachment to abundance." When clutter occupies spaces, countertops, and corners of your environment, this can make you feel overwhelmed, drained, and stressed out. Anything that stresses you out or zaps your energy will inevitably interfere with your connection to Spirit.

Just as you might quickly pick up around the house before a friend visits, think of it as the same with Spirit. Take a moment to recycle the stacks of mail on the counter and put away the shoes and socks on the floor. I always find it interesting that when you start cleaning up one area, you suddenly notice other things along the way. If you're overwhelmed trying to find permanent places for things, the best thing you can do is find some type of organizer or storage container. Start with one area at a time, setting clear guidelines and realistic expectations for yourself, such as one drawer a day. Do this enough times, and you'll start to call your energy back. One will seep quite naturally into the next. As soon as I start picking up papers off my desk, I find that I have cleared the space, and I end the process by lighting some non-synthetic incense. Then I strike my crystal sound bowl to clear out the final remnants of energetic clutter. I can energetically notice the difference. You'll be surprised how practices such as decluttering your space to invite Spirit in can make an enormous difference in your ability to connect. Be sure to watch out for things you can't close, like overstuffed drawers, trunks, boxes, closets, the trunk of your car. If you can't close it, clean it! If you are having trouble, it may be because you have emotions to be processed around these items. When these emotions are left unresolved, they can turn into attachments.

ATTACHMENTS

If you want to understand what you're attached to, think of what really makes you angry and what you dislike or find distasteful. So if you absolutely hate going to the gym, then you likely have an attachment to it; if you hate paying bills, attachment; don't like the way your boss treats you, attachment; feel really annoyed or envious when you see couples kissing or holding hands, attachment. You get the point. An attachment is a state of suffering. It's when you can't stop ruminating or revisiting things that you believe have upset, rattled, hurt, or took something from you. In other words, if you don't go to the gym, then the chances of getting out of shape or feeling crappy about yourself may increase. As this occurs, you may get anxious or depressed over it. Therefore, it may not be that you really dislike the gym but more so the feeling of what may happen if you don't.

Here's the thing: attachment is something you absolutely dislike and maybe even resent feeling; this is why attachments seem to go wherever we do. Perhaps you really dislike being single or the feeling you had when your old boyfriend cheated on you. So attachments are likely something you are meant to work through rather than attach to. When I asked Spirit about attachments, I was reminded of other ways we create this suffering. Spirit brought to my attention the way we attach to the unknown or uncertainty. For example, when you experience physical symptoms such as bodily pain or a skin rash, you immediately want to know what the cause is so you can fix it.

Yet, when neither the cause nor the solution can be found, this may cause you to attach to it even more. While some people may stumble upon spontaneous discoveries, remedies, and even cures through researching and studying their alignments, it seems the energy of your inquiry can really make a difference. In other words, if you are coming from a place of curiosity, inspiration, or passion, then this will influence the way the energy moves in your body. Yet if you come from a place of panic, anger, disbelief, or shock (like my client Maria) when you ask Spirit, then this too will reflect in your energy centers. It is not that one is necessarily better than the other but more so how it can promote a state of suffering.

If you're wondering how to overcome or transform these types of reactions, the answer is to become aware and trust that from this point forward, the remaining chapters in this book will provide that information. For now, these are just things I need you to be aware of, especially when it comes to connecting to and working with energy. Therefore, I would be remiss if I didn't mention other types of attachments such as energy attachments.

ENERGY ATTACHMENTS

Years ago, I was trained in *Reiki* energy healing, which is an ancient Japanese healing modality that moves energy around the body. Reiki means universal life energy. Once I began to see clients, there were several times after giving a treatment that my energy would feel zapped. Basically, I would do Reiki and then go home and take a nap. I remember thinking, *I have got to get some additional training*. Spirit clearly heard me because the next thing I know I'm in a clothing boutique and the clerk starts chatting with me about this energy healer in town, telling me I should get to know her as we have a lot in common. I called this energy healer the same day, and she said, "I have a class in quantum healing tomorrow. Do you want to join?" I replied, "Yes!" I attended the class not knowing we would be learning all about removing energy attachments!

Energy attachments don't have a body. Instead, they are more like an entity that only has interests of its own. Energy attachments do not serve you at all; they take from you. Energy attachments can arrive in thought forms, come from past or present relationships, live in physical (typically heavy, dense, low vibrational) spaces, and even arrive from different dimensions or worlds. They can also come in the form of a psychic attack. A psychic attack is when someone or a group of people wish ill will on you. Sometimes this can come across as unprocessed jealousy or envy. Many people have had energy attachments and never even knew it. While this can seem a little scary, I'd like to think this is what it looks like to be part of a universe. The good news is, it's all energy, and through chakra work, emotional processing, reciting mantras, and connection to divine Spirit, you can not only protect yourself but clear your energy.

Think of energy attachments like this: if your immune system is low and you walk in a room where someone is sick with a cold, the chances of you picking up that cold are greater than if you walked in healthy and strong. For some of my clients whose occupation is to go into these heavy spaces on a regular basis—law enforcement agents, health and human services providers, addiction counselors—this often leads to a higher rate of burnout than another jobs. The good news is that the tools, strategies, Cleanses, and suggestions I offer in this book, combined with supports such as therapy, nutrition, and/ or exercise, can help. Here are some signs of an energy attachment:

SIGNS OF ENERGY ATTACHMENT
Low energy or chronic fatigue
Strange dreams or altered sleep patterns
Mood swings (for example, impulsive anger) that are out of character
Suicidal or dark thoughts
A gut feeling that something doesn't feel right or that you picked up on something negative
Hearing voices (aural hallucinations)
Addictions (alcohol, drugs, social media, shopping, porn)

Energy attachments can also happen from careless, random sex, overdosing on social media, living among individuals suffering with depression or addiction, overworking, or being influenced by cult-like behavior. Here's the interesting part: the more you clear your energy, the lighter you become. As a result, you likely make some changes to your internal and external environment. For example, I've never been a big drinker, but I found hanging on to the one occasional glass of wine didn't really serve me. No judgment here; it's how my body works. I also no longer feel guilty if I don't keep in constant contact with individuals who may be negative or have a lot of drama in their life. The reality is, what doesn't serve you likely doesn't serve anyone else either, so let it go.

As I mentioned earlier, I lead a weekly virtual membership. This is a sacred space where I encourage everyone to focus on light, and we do a bit of what I call Soul Cleansing. This means we work with the soul as guide for what and how to Cleanse. Each week I offer tools (like the ones in this book), and together we put them into practice. Being part of a group is like having an accountability partner. If you feel as if your energy or aura is weak, or if you just want to expand your energy, then I highly encourage you to check out Membership at sheriannaboyle.com/membership. Which leads me to another way your connection to Spirit becomes weak, and that is through spiritual bypassing.

SPIRITUAL BYPASSING

Those of us who identify as being more spiritual (like me) than religious often feel like we're not taken as seriously. We can at times be looked upon as spiritual bypassing, which is another way of saying we use spirituality as a way to avoid, cover up, or ignore our problems. Yet when I received the question, *What emotions are you avoiding?* from Spirit, it got me thinking. Most people don't avoid feelings of fear, insecurity, doubt, and worry. They don't even avoid feelings of rejection, disappointment, or shame; I find what most people avoid feeling . . . is love.

When we avoid love, in my opinion we are spiritual bypassing. Many of us avoid feeling love as a way to protect ourselves from getting hurt, feeling vulnerable, rejected, or sad. Some ways I have seen this occur is when someone chooses to hold a grudge or project (bitch, complain, blame) their pain onto others. Where it gets cloudy is sometimes these behaviors are reinforced by society, with a "screw them" mentality. "You go, girl, let 'em have it, don't let people treat you that way." While I am all for empowering one another to stand up for what is right, when I lean into the Rays of Light, I receive guidance that looks and feels quite different. By taking part in regular emotional Cleanses, connecting with Spirit, and practicing ways to enhance my intuition, I find little to no room for diversion. The spiritual path is not about punishing yourself or anyone else. It is a discipline.

There are more ways to enhance your connection to Spirit. Let's take a look at them in the next chapter. But before moving on, take a moment to get to know the sixth step of the Cleanse: *S* for Surrender.

CLEANSE HIGHLIGHT: S, SURRENDER

S in the Cleanse stands for surrender. The purpose of this step is to give yourself permission to fully let go and trust the true power, resiliency, of yourself as a Spiritual being in a human body. By doing so, you are holding yourself 100 percent accountable for not only what you feel, think, and believe but also any patterns, habits, or dynamics. To surrender means you are choosing with your own free will to no longer force, fix, control, or manage what is happening or what you're feeling. This is how it looks and feels to be fully accountable.

The way this step works is through repeating affirmations out loud, such as *I allow balance. I allow spiritual cleansing. I allow attention.* Surrendering and being accountable lets your spiritual team know that you're consciously on the path to learning the lessons, understandings, and knowledge you've come to Earth to learn. It also helps you retrain your subconscious mind so that you no longer block, resist, or minimize what you feel.

CHAPTER 7

AMPLIFY YOUR CONNECTION

In Spirit everything is connected
and happens at once.

I was in the middle of planning an international retreat. Normally, I get asked to speak and teach at retreat centers, yet with this particular retreat, I was required to get ten sign-ups before it could happen. I was at nine. Just when I got to ten and thought I was all set, a person canceled. This happened two more times, nine, ten, cancel. I turned to Spirit for help. "Spirit," I said, "I need some reassurance this is all going to work out. Can you send me a sign?" Within minutes, I see a license plate with the number 222, and it brings a smile to my face. The previous evening, I had been shopping online, and my order number came back with the number 2222. Only a few minutes later as I drove down the road, the next 222 arrived. But what did it all mean?

Then this happened: I felt a wave of gratitude. I thought to myself, *Rather than be upset about not having ten, be grateful for those nine. You have nine people; celebrate that.* Shifting my energy and attention in this way brought about a feeling of lightness. The next day, I received an e-mail letting me know the order number 2222 did not go through and that I needed to call the main number. I called the number, and they said, "Oh, order number 2222, I had to adjust your payment, it went through today." Talk about reassurance!

What enhances your connection to Spirit is trust. Nothing brings you more ease than trust. The message of the number 222 and seeing multiples of the numeral 2 carries the frequency of harmony, balance, precision, service, and manifestation. Two fosters unity and cooperation, and also encourages you to transform any fearful negative thinking into positive energy for growth. Once my energy became lighter and I began to appreciate the nine, I realized the retreat was in perfect balance: everyone on the retreat knew someone. It felt to me as if Spirit was saying that this is the perfect amount for me to experience this retreat with effortlessness and ease. As these signs came in, I was able to let go and trust this was all happening in my favor as well as in the best interest of everyone else attending.

What enhances your connection? It could be faith, vulnerability, authenticity, sacred rituals, and spiritual amplifiers, such as adding crystals.

FAITH

I have come across many people over the years who've lost faith in themselves, one another, and even humanity altogether. When this occurs, the experience can often be accompanied by a pervading bitterness, disgust, anger, or unexpressed sadness. As a result, some people may find themselves moving in and out of depression, or they view their lives as a string of bad luck or a never-ending cycle of roadblocks or pitfalls. With all this, I've noticed a persistent occupation with the finite can set in.

By finite, I mean a fixed way of looking at things. As human beings without awareness, our minds can become quite caught up with deadlines, endings, outcomes, benchmarks, goals, measurements, sales, and numbers. For example, you might hear yourself say things like "This is my last day at work" or "This is the last holiday celebrated in this way." Another way this appears is when you overfocus on the number of calories you eat or get down about how much money is in your bank account.

Should these things happen, as they do, this is a sign, darling, that you're losing energy big-time. Trust that just by asking Spirit to come around, you'll be lifted up again. Then pay attention to the signs and synchronicities. If you don't see them, this doesn't mean they're not there; it simply means you're more focused on the finite (the outcome) than the infinite.

This reminds me of a client who once asked how I was so certain there was eternal life and that we didn't really die. My response was because spirits come into my sessions all the time. They tell me things I would have never known, and when I share these things with the client, they get emotional recognizing the connection. When Spirit is around, I feel things more deeply, including sensations such as love and compassion. I have worked with people who have done horrible things (lying, cheating, stealing, crimes, abuse), but when Spirit is with me, I can see both the good in them and their potential. This gives me hope and faith. This will happen as you ask and receive from Spirit. Having hope is underrated. It's an emotion that liberates you from finite thinking while softening the edges between transitions. Rather than stop, worry, and move to the next thing, you pause, take in, and allow yourself to be guided.

There is a Kundalini yoga chant that illustrates this beautifully: sa-ta-na-ma. In Sanskrit, sa means infinity, ta means life, na means death, and ma means rebirth. Should you be overly consumed or distracted by details, chanting sa-ta-na-ma out loud is a gentle way to detach from the fear of endings (the "what-if") and instead remain focused and centered on what is.

Yet if you choose to continue down the path of finite thinking, this would be an awfully convenient way to avoid feeling anything, wouldn't it? Here's the thing: there are going to be many times in life when you won't understand why things are the way they are. You won't be able to control the speed or intensity of what is happening. Yet through emotional processing and the tools in this book, what you can do is ask Spirit to come a little closer, to huddle around you as you move through these challenging and at times inevitable transitions.

It's like when I met with Robert. He was in the middle of getting ready for his aging mother to transition to a new home closer to his house so he could help take care of her. Since the home his mother was selling had been in the family for over fifty years, this transition came with its fair share of sadness and grief. I could tell Robert was focused on the finite as he kept repeating the phrase, "This might be our last." Like "This might be our last Thanksgiving" or "This might be the last birthday we celebrate together." I encouraged Robert to soften his grip around the idea of things being finite and instead learn to embrace the infinite. When Robert approached it from the finite, he was more likely to try to manage the transition and his emotions. Yet, when he focused on the infinite, he gave himself permission to accept the situation fully as is. After moving through a couple of Cleanses, Robert and I developed a plan. When he and his mother became stressed, he would place his hand on his heart, encourage his mother to do the same, and together they would connect to the infinite and breathe. Of course, this suggestion made Robert feel a bit vulnerable, which (believe it or not!) is another way you enhance your connection to Spirit.

VULNERABILITY

Robert, a young man who had recently applied to several colleges, booked a session with me. When I asked him how I could help, he said he needed help manifesting the right college. "Did you already apply?" I inquired. "Yes," he said.

"Okay, then you are in the waiting period, right?" I responded.

"Yes," he said.

"Then I'm not going to help you manifest which one; what I can do, however, is help you sit in the discomfort of not knowing what is going to happen."

I knew helping him process the emotions around the discomfort of waiting would serve him far more than giving him some manifesting affirmations or practices. You see, what we don't always recognize are the ways our discomfort can be a sign of growth. With growth comes expansion, and with expansion comes Spirit.

A few months after our meeting, Robert contacted me with great news, yet he wasn't quite sure how it happened. "Sherianna," he said, "I got into a college I never should have gotten into."

"What do you mean?" I asked.

"Well," he said, "it had a 7 percent acceptance rate, and there is no way my grades were good enough."

"Remember," I said, "we asked Spirit to help you get into the college that was for your greatest and highest good. There you go, you got it!"

Here's the thing: it isn't always comfortable to be in transition, head in a new direction, give up old habits, share your true feelings, move, or step into the unknown. When these things occur, it can make you feel overwhelmed, nervous, and vulnerable. What you may not realize is this vulnerability is often the birthplace for new beginnings. Not just new things or experiences but also states of being. With my years of experience as a coach, I've learned that vulnerability means you are right on the cusp of stepping into authenticity and higher potential. When you embrace it, vulnerability can be a powerful surge of vibration that allows you to move the energy from your upper body and chakra system to the lower body, or vice versa.

In Robert's case, what I noticed was his energy was open from the heart up. In other words, his higher spiritual chakras (heart, throat, third eye, and crown) were strong, yet from the heart down, I told him it was like he had no legs. Energetically, his lower chakras (solar plexus, sacral, and root) were moving much slower. Think of it as a plant that is sprouting aboveground, but underneath the surface (the part you can't see), the roots are brittle. To get the legs, I encouraged him to put his hands on his lower belly and take slow deep breaths, inhaling and exhaling as he directed his awareness to his lower body: hips, legs, and feet. Become the director of your own energy, I said, learn how to turn Spirit (breath) into a resource for distributing energy throughout your entire being.

Through practices such as these, your understanding and experience with vulnerability will expand—you'll no longer view it as a weakness but instead recognize it for what it is: *a temporary escalation of energy in motion.* As your vibration energy increases in awareness you may sense an increase of thoughts, or a tightness (sometimes experienced as tension) in energy. In those moments, it may help to refer to the words of author Brené Brown, who said in her often-quoted 2012 TED Talk, "Vulnerability is the birthplace of innovation, creativity, and change." Through vulnerability, you can discover your authentic self.

AUTHENTICITY

When there is energy moving throughout your entire body, you feel relaxed and safe. This sense of safety is what gives you the means to live from a place of honesty and authenticity. Think of enhancing your relationship with Spirit the way you might strengthen other relationships in your life. When you're genuine and honest, your relationships have more of a chance to gain stable ground. When these qualities are present, our energetic system is allowed to relax and expand. Yet when there are untruths, lies, or agendas, our nervous systems can go off-kilter, and as this occurs, we lose our connection to Spirit. This can make you feel unloved, unappreciated, and unsupported. To be in connection with Spirit on a regular basis means to choose to balance and expand your energy on a regular basis.

When it comes to asking Spirit for guidance, support, love, and clarity, Spirit knows (just like I did with the young man wanting to manifest the right college) when you are trying to control or manipulate energy. When things don't happen right away or the way we want, it can be easy to take things personally (even from Spirit). The reality is we don't cultivate authenticity from fixing or managing the next thing. When you choose to feel first and then ask (receive), you experience Spirit as everything.

In these states, when mind, body, and your Spirit are one, you can speak your truth. This means energetically you can state how you feel, or sit in an experience of disappointment, fear, even anger without losing energy. This means you can feel the energetic vibration of anger without reacting to it. Or you can experience the vibration of sadness, hurt, or shame without turning to external sources or distractions as a way to cope. Instead, you consciously choose to open yourself up to vulnerability and to experience your emotions as raw and pure without needing to taint them with the narratives or stories they often carry.

One of the shortest verses in the King James Bible is John 11:35, which simply says, "Jesus wept." While there are many interpretations of that verse, to me it shows Jesus Christ's vulnerability and authenticity. When we weep, or tear up, it's often a sign of our humanness and how much we really care. It can also be an indication of how deep our love can go. When we choose to include sacred rituals in our lives, we are choosing to foster high spiritual qualities within ourselves by focusing on meaning, purpose, and devotion.

SACRED RITUALS

Before describing a sacred ritual, let me tell you the difference between a ritual and a routine. Routines are habits. When I get up in the morning, I might have the routine of brushing my teeth or getting a drink of water. Oh, who am I kidding, coffee always comes first! Rituals tend to have more of an emotional connection or meaning. I don't have an emotional connection to my toothbrush; it's more a matter of taking care of my teeth to prevent future problems. But each morning when I sit in my armchair with a fresh cup of coffee on the table next to me and a large chunk of rose quartz in the palm of my hands and mala beads around my neck, I am in ritual. This is me choosing to raise my vibration so that I can connect to my emotions, spiritual guides, archangels, and ascended beings.

Like routines, rituals are repeated. Routines are typically done without much thought or awareness. Perhaps you have the routine of watching television before you go to sleep or taking your shoes off before you enter your home. Rituals, on the other hand, are performed out of devotion and often include a sacred object, certain phrases, songs, chants, or movements.

For example, you might have a ritual of lighting a candle each morning as a way to invite your guides in. You may have a ritual of carrying around or wearing a sacred item (a cross around your neck, medal of a saint, or something to remind you of a loved one). Or maybe you have tattoos that represent your beliefs, people you love, scripture, lyrics, or verses that represent your Spirit connection.

When it comes to the Chakra Cleanses in Part 3, you could pair each Cleanse with a sacred object such as a crystal. A list of crystals and their corresponding chakras follows. Just note a sacred object doesn't need to be purchased. It can be a rock you found on the beach that called to you, a feather, shell, picture of a loved one, or a statue of an ascended being. Some people even create sacred altars, a special place where their sacred items remain displayed and tended to. For example, you may have a ritual of lighting incense around your sacred items as a way to show respect and refresh the energy.

I once purchased a Buddha statue that came from a sacred temple. The instructions that came with the statue were to share a piece of food (like a piece of fruit) or water with it every day as a form of *saddha* (devotion, faith). Believe it or not, I kept my word and did this devotional practice—until I didn't. After missing the ritual for several days, I called the vendor and asked if I could sell it back as I was unable to keep my promise. He bought it back, and in the same day someone else who had a love of Buddha purchased it. Therefore, whatever ritual you create, be sure it's one that is realistic.

Rather than a statue, I now have some crystal angels on my altar. Crystals are solids (often, but not always, minerals) with a highly organized, repeating arrangement of atoms, molecules, or ions. This arrangement creates various geometric patterns, which many believe promote different qualities and characteristics (such as harmony, peace, balance, clearing) depending on the specific crystal. When moving through the Chakra Cleanse, it can be nice to have a crystal nearby or in the palm of your hand as a sacred ritual for raising your vibration. You may even choose to wear crystals or keep one in your pocket. I have a friend who keeps a substantial chunk of lapis lazuli in her bra (she is supersensitive to energy). Regardless of the reason, be sure you have a piece of selenite around as well; this helps keep your crystals clear because they can absorb energy from the environment.

❀

It's believed by some that holding crystals or positioning them on various areas of the body can give physical and mental benefits. The idea is that crystals interact with the body's energy field, creating balance and alignment (Meg Walters, Healthline).

Radios and watches were once powered by crystals. Think about crystals similarly working with your body.

Here are some crystals you might consider incorporating into your Chakra Cleanses:

CRYSTALS AND THEIR RELATED CHAKRAS	
Crown chakra	Clear quartz
Third eye	Amethyst
Throat	Lapis lazuli
Heart	Green aventurine
Solar plexus	Tiger's eye
Sacral chakra	Moonstone
Root chakra	Red jasper

CLEANSE HIGHLIGHT: *E,* EASE

The last step of the Cleanse is *E,* for ease. This comes from the embodiment of the "I am" presence. This happens by transforming your "I allow" statements into "I am" statements. The "I am" appears 957 times in the King James Bible (Revised Standard Version). Some healers, spiritual teachers, and religious leaders believe these are the two most powerful words you can repeat.

The purpose of this step is to integrate yourself as mind, body, and Spirit. When you repeat "I am" phrases, you are no longer separate from Source. In this step, I encourage you to claim your "I amness." It is the difference between saying, "I allow the Holy Spirit" to "I am the Holy Spirit" or "I allow worthy" to "I am worthy." This helps you remember that you are a perfect creation of God.

CHANNELING

To channel means to become a conduit for Spirit. If you have ever had a moment when you were inspired to write down an idea or even song lyrics that popped into your mind out of nowhere, you know what I mean. In Part 2, we will explore different ways to channel information from Spirit. They include breathing, meditating, Spirit writing, Spirit walks, autonomic coloring, and more. At the end of each chapter, I share some Spirit messages: little pieces of guidance Spirit has provided to me along the way.

CHAPTER 8

CLEARING PATTERNS: SACRED BREATH

The human spirit lives on creativity and
dies in conformity and routine.

—Vilayat Inayat

While I was writing this book, I asked my psychic-medium friend Anna if she thought *Just Ask Spirit* would be picked up by a publisher. Normally, I feel confident about these things, but for whatever reason, I felt a little nudge to ask. As usual, Anna took my set of car keys and after a long inhale and then a very slow and deliberate exhale, she dropped down into what she referred to as alpha brain wave

states. It is not unusual for a psychic medium to ask for an item with
your energy on it (like a wedding ring or car keys) to channel Spirit.

Within seconds she took a breath and said, "I have a man named
James here. He says, 'I can see it on many shelves,' and he shows me
pictures of bookshelves."

That would be my father-in-law. Although we weren't close when
he was on earth, he seems to be the one who shows up most often
when I get a reading from her. What I later realized is James was not
only giving me reassurance but he was also teaching me how to manifest (your guides will do this now and then). He knew if he shared
it in that way, I would start to visualize it on many shelves, and this
would help it to materialize physically. Pretty clever, huh? He was
very much known for being clever, along with being a great teacher. I
always find it pretty cool how even in Spirit, our loved ones continue
to share their guidance in recognizable ways.

Yet, what can happen as you channel is, as the information kicks
in, old fears or anxieties can begin to surface. For example, hearing
the information that it would be on many shelves might bring up a
feeling of fear or anxiety because the pressure is on. This is normal
and common in channeling stuff, when beliefs and fearful or worrisome thoughts can come up. Not to worry; many of the tools and
practices to improve your ability to channel can also be useful for
clearing patterns.

CLEARING PATTERNS

In yoga we refer to patterns as samskaras.

The word samskara derives from the Sanskrit *sam* (complete
or joined together) and *kara* (action, cause, or doing). It is
commonly translated as "mental impression," "habit pattern,"

or "recollection." They rest in the unconscious inner self and form the basic inner drives that influence and effect future actions (Yoga Basics).

Most of these habits are unconscious and can influence the way we react to one another as well as the information we receive from Spirit. You will see how this all comes together, in Part 3, as a practice. For now, it is important for you to get to know these ancient practices, as they help you get to know yourself so you can fully align with your purpose.

BREATH

You can use breathing to focus on creating space in your body by expanding your lungs and lower belly. The breath is an essential way to clear up the samskaras. One way to do this is to divide your breath into three parts. When you breathe in, slowly inflate your lower belly like a balloon. As you inhale, your diaphragm contracts downward making space for more air to enter your chest, and as you exhale, your diaphragm relaxes.

Be sure to sit or stand up tall when breathing. To further nurture this process, count to three as you inhale and exhale.

Inhale . . . one . . . two . . . three . . . exhale . . . one . . . two . . . three . . .

Each time you breathe in and out, picture your lungs in your mind as you count. You are inflating one, the lower part of your lungs; two, the middle; and three, upper lungs. Then exhale completely—relax. Repeat this several times in a row and notice how this promotes a sense of calm and relaxation throughout your entire body. As you do this, your breath becomes a vehicle for connecting to your higher self.

Before taking part in any breathing exercise, or breath retention or holding exercises, please consult with your
doctor, especially if you are pregnant or have any respiratory conditions, a history of seizures, epilepsy, heart conditions, asthma, or any other health concerns. Be careful and
never do them while driving or during an ice water plunge.

HIGHER-SELF BREATHING

Connecting to your higher self on a daily basis is an essential skill
for clearing and opening the pathway for channeling. When you are
connected to your higher self, you'll know because you feel more
open, calm, at times tingly (vibration), and present. There are two
ways to access your higher self through breathing: One is to stretch
your breath out by breathing one or two counts longer when you inhale, and the second is to introduce a little bit of *breath retention*. You
can also combine the two together. The practice of breath retention,
also known in yoga as *kumbhaka*, means that you hold the breath
briefly before exhaling or inhaling, depending on the practice.

By taking part in such practices, you increase *prana* (breath) in
your body. In Sanskrit prana means life-force energy. Essentially,
you're creating a current of energy. The word *nadi* literally means
flow or current. Nadis are subtle energy channels in which the
pranic force flows. This process is spoken about in the ancient Vedic
text called the *Upanishads*. The *Upanishads* share vital information
about the universe and the process of manifestation. According to
Dr. Marc Halpern, founder and president of the California College
of Ayurveda, there are 72,000 nadis in the psychic body. Through

breathing practices, you can activate psychic (channeling) and healing abilities, unlocking your higher potential to both give and receive energy—and messages—from the divine.

Here are some more ways to stretch and expand your breath potential.

Rooting Breath

This is a great breath practice for beginners. It can be done either by sitting up tall in a comfortable position or lying down flat on your back. With rooting breath, picture roots of a tree going deep within Mother Earth. As the roots extend, this gives you an overall sense of calm, safety, and security. Picture the roots going down and across the earth as you breathe in slowly through your nose (inflating your lower abdominal area for the count of three), and then on the exhale through your nose, slowly making your breath one or two counts longer.

- It will look something like this: inhale, inflate your lower belly (one, two, three), and exhale, deflate pushing your navel toward your spine, four, three, two, one. You may add a little breath retention in between to give it a little bit more of a grounding effect.

- When it comes to asking Spirit, you can ask your question and then do this type of breathing technique five to ten times in a row. Then release and let yourself receive the answers. Adding a little breath retention helps you surrender any resistance. In Part 3, where I share the Cleanses, you can try out these different types of breathing styles, during the N, nourish (channeling), portion of the Cleanse.

Chakra Breathing

Your chakras are part of your anatomy of Spirit. Besides colors, each chakra is represented by petals of a flower. Please visit sheriannaboyle.com, at the *Just Ask Spirit* book page, to find a *free* downloadable image of the mandalas related to your chakras. With chakra breathing, you imagine the petals of each chakra opening up and contracting one at a time. Think of the petals as flexible and in motion, like the energy in your lungs as they expand and contract. When it comes to asking Spirit, this is how you want to work with your own energy. When you're connecting, you'll open your energy up, and then when you go about your daily life (for example, doing errands), allow the energy to relax and contract a bit. This will help you feel more balanced.

When it comes to Part 3, you will see how each Cleanse corresponds to your chakra centers. It can help to place your attention onto one chakra as you breathe. When you inhale, imagine the part of your body where that chakra is located. Visualize that area as the corresponding colors and petals of a flower opening wide to Spirit, and on the exhale, imagine the petals relaxing and closing inward as the exhale draws the information closer to you in the physical realm. Here are the colors of each chakra along with the number of petals associated with each one.

CHAKRA COLORS		
White	Crown chakra	1,000-plus petals
Violet	Third-eye chakra	two petals
Blue	Throat chakra	sixteen petals
Green	Heart chakra	twelve petals
Yellow	Solar plexus chakra	ten petals
Orange	Sacral chakra	six petals
Red	Root chakra	four petals

It is said that the archangels look over our chakras. Deborah Lloyd, Reiki Master and author of *22 Messages from Archangels* as well as the *Archangels and the Chakras* pdf guide, is one of them. In Part 3, you will see the 7777 Pathways, Cleansing with the archangels, in which I have matched each archangel according to their corresponding chakra.

Aura Breathing

An aura is an invisible energy field that surrounds all living things. It is said that your aura has seven layers (just as you have seven main chakras) and within the aura and chakras both positive and negative energies can be stored. When it comes to aura breathing you may find different techniques out there. I describe below the one I use most frequently and teach to my students and clients.

To begin, place your attention on your heart center. Then place your palms together in front of your heart space and start rubbing them vigorously together. As you do this, take short and quick inhales and exhales. Inhale, one count, and exhale, one count. You will snap your belly back quickly on exhale. It can help to rub your hands together to the beat of your breath.

Breathe in and out this way five to ten times in a row, pause, then pull the palms of your hands gently apart, yet keep them close enough so you can sense and feel the pulsing of the energy between your hands. Once you do, start to gently pull your palms farther apart, stretching the energy outward into your aura. When your arms are fully extended, flip your palms outward as if to motion the energy to keep flowing outward. If you lose connection to the energy, rub your hands together again while doing one-to-one breathing (*inhale, one count . . . exhale, one count . . .*). If you can't do that type of breathing due to a medical condition, do this exercise with the rubbing of the hands and keep the breath flowing naturally.

Don't be surprised if you see, sense, or feel many colors in your auric field during this exercise. If so, allow yourself to bask in this rainbow light. When you end the practice, connect your hands in front of your heart in a prayer position with the intention to create a balanced energy field and to connect the right and left hemispheres of your brain.

Reset and Refresh Breath: Left Nostril Breathing

Sometimes we get so caught up in the physical, whether our life is or is not flowing in the way we were hoping it would. This is when you can benefit from a reset. If so, I have two tips: One, take a break from social media, and two, do the reset and refresh breath practice. This is a wonderful way to reconnect to your spiritual roots and soul purpose. It's also called left nostril breathing.

In terms of asking Spirit, if you're feeling desperate for support, advice, or guidance, do yourself a favor and do this reset before you ask. This helps close the gap between you and Spirit.

I've seen it many times, and other yoga teachers have shared with me as well how effective this practice can be. This breath practice is best performed by sitting up tall in a comfortable seated position. First, take a moment to relax your body by taking one or two slow, deep breaths. Be sure your spine and neck are long, and shoulders are relaxed. This breath practice is like counting the breath only, instead, using your dominant hand, you block off the right nostril with your right thumb, so you are exclusively breathing through your left nostril. The left nostril is known to specifically send feedback to your parasympathetic nervous system (the part of your nervous system that calms you down). You may have to blow your nose to clear the passageway before taking part.

- Close off your right nostril and breathe through the left, inflating your lower abdomen at the same time. *Inhale . . . one . . . two . . . three . . . exhale . . . one . . . two . . . three . . . four. . . .*
- Hold the breath for three seconds and *exhale . . . one . . . two . . . three . . . four. . . .*
- You may also count higher or change up the ratio as you become more comfortable with this breath technique. *Inhale . . . one . . . two . . . three . . . four . . . exhale . . . one . . . two . . . three . . . four . . . five. Pause. Exhale six . . . five . . . four . . . three . . . two . . . one. . . .*
- Begin with breathing this way for thirty seconds, and work your way up to two minutes or more.

Light Me Up! Circular (Open Mouth) Breathing

Lastly, we have "Light me up!" breath. This is my go-to practice when I feel like I want to kick some butt in terms of knocking down some of those perceived obstacles (fears, worries) in my life once and for all. Since it requires keeping your mouth open the entire time, you truly do have to be up for this practice. Depending on the length of time I choose to do it for, I will sometimes play some upbeat music in the background to keep me going.

With this breathing technique your mouth is open the entire time. Inhale through your mouth, inflating your lower abdominal area, pause briefly (two or three seconds), and then exhale pulling your navel toward your spine through your mouth. Again, never hold your breath or do any vigorous breathing if you're pregnant or have any other contraindications such as respiratory difficulties, asthma, heart disease, epilepsy, history of seizures, glaucoma, vertigo, and more. Your mouth will get dry as you do this technique. Since it can be uncomfortable to hold your mouth open, it can help to lie down during this practice.

The length of your practice is up to you. Unless you're working with a trained breathwork facilitator, start slowly (about one minute or less) and work up to longer periods of time (several minutes). Rather than counting your breath, let it flow freely in and out, taking in and releasing as much air as you like. Your breathing will be a bit noisy, and if it feels right, feel free to make whatever noises you want on exhale. Some people make the sound of ahh as they exhale. No need to be embarrassed here. There's no right or wrong here, as long as you are taking air (oxygen) in and releasing carbon dioxide out of your lungs.

If you choose to do a longer (for example, five minutes or more) circular (open mouth) breath, don't operate any kind of motor vehicle immediately after. Give yourself some time to get fully back into your body, an hour or so, before you operate a motor vehicle as you might feel a bit lightheaded afterward.

My Spirit Message: Change Your Water

This message came to me in the form of an image of a vase of flowers. Here's the interpretation of what I received from Spirit:

"Think of your breath like a vase of flowers. After a few days if you don't change it, the water in the vase will likely become murky. When left in this way bacteria forms. This impacts how much hydration the stems of the flowers can take in, and this is why you see dead leaves form. Your breath changes your water. When you add intention into your practice, your breath becomes the abundant resource of life-force energy. Intention is about carrying out love, service, purpose, and truth. Focus less on getting rid of old stale energy and more on the intention of what you are carrying out when you breathe. Everything serves a greater purpose in the Spirit world."

CHAPTER 9

BE STILL AND KNOW: MEDITATION

Meditation is a process of lighting up,
of trusting the basic goodness of what we have and
who we are, and of realizing any wisdom that exists,
exists in what we already have.

—Pema Chodron

"Silence" followed by *"Be still and know that I am there"* is the response I heard when I asked Archangel Raphael how to teach people to connect to their guides and spiritual team. Since my visitation from Archangel Raphael (yes, I had a visitation) several weeks prior, I found my interest in meditation increased while activities

that weakened my vibration decreased. For example, I had a strange shift around a couple of relationships. In other words, I gave myself permission to release someone who had been pulling on me energetically. It wasn't the fact that I released this person, which amazed me, but more so in my ability to do it with love. This would all make sense later.

The visitation was quite surprising (there's that surprise thing again); after all, who expects something like that to happen? He (yes, I experienced it more as a masculine energy) came to me in my sleep, after I called on him before I went to bed and asked him to help heal my ears. I was experiencing some very annoying ear ringing.

While the ear ringing did not stop completely, the visitation led me to research things like the relationship between caffeine, alcohol, and tinnitus. Since the visitation was such a powerful experience, I felt that the two were connected. The symptoms have not disappeared yet, but the stress and anxiety I was having around the ringing did, to the point where it no longer impacted my mood and levels of fatigue.

In my book *Energy in Action*, I pair Archangel Raphael with the spiritual law of compensation. What I learned about this law through connecting to Spirit is that when you choose to surrender, let go, your energy moves, and you're compensated with new energy, insights, support, and guidance.

In Part 3, after Cleansing, I encourage you to ask Spirit by writing down a question before meditating. This can be a request to have one of your spiritual team members come be with you, or a specific request such as *Help me to heal my anxiety around* _____ *or to overcome my fear of* _____.

If you're concerned you may be asking the "wrong" guide or Spirit to assist you, know they all work together in Spirit. So, if you call on an ascended being like Mother Mary or your guardian angel, don't be surprised if you sense more than one guide around you. This is because there's no ego in Spirit. Guides don't compete with one another for attention like humans do. Instead, they live in harmony with one another and come from pure unconditional love. Just ask!

Once you put your question out there, then you may choose the option in Part 3 to meditate to receive the energy of Spirit. Remember, in Spirit everything happens at once. There is no wait time. Consider it done even if it has not materialized yet. The following meditation practices not only help you prepare for Part 3 but also can help you develop your channeling abilities outside of Cleansing.

WHAT IS MEDITATION?

Meditation has been around for more than 5,000 years and can be found integrated into many world religions, philosophies, cultures, and yoga traditions. The benefits of meditation have been well researched and, as a result, it has become one of the most highly recommended practices for helping you process your emotions and change your brain, thereby improving memory and decreasing stress.

If you're someone who just doesn't see yourself as a meditator, maybe you're a parent of small children, work long hours, or consider yourself an anxious person, I hear you.

With the Cleanses offered in Part 3 (the 7777 Pathways), you can meditate as little or as long as you like. With that said, if you have a busy lifestyle like me, I look for consistency and quality versus quantity. Strive for five to ten minutes a day or a few times a week. Maybe it's in the morning as you sip your first cup of coffee or a moment of quiet after taking your shower. Meditation is simply a way to quiet your mind and be in the present moment.

As you increase and maintain these calmer states, you'll begin to notice the ways your spiritual team is with you. For example, when teaching online, I guided participants into a meditation after invoking the presence of Archangel Raphael. As I was guiding the students I could feel the presence of Archangel Raphael with me, so much that I stated out loud, "Archangel Raphael is with us, and is encouraging you to surrender all your worries and fears, let them go, and he will assist you." I repeated this a few times, and then in what felt like a fraction of a second, there was a huge shift of consciousness. As the participants let go of resistance, a beautiful green light came shining through—I could clearly see it and feel it in my mind's eye.

After the meditation, one of the participants asked me if I was playing ocean sounds in the background. I said no. She said she kept hearing the ocean, and it felt like beautiful music. Another participant who wasn't in the live meditation but instead watched the recorded replay reached out to let me know he could see, sense, and feel the aura of Archangel Raphael.

Remember that the S in Cleanse stands for surrender. Although it sounds contradictory, there's a lot of power in surrender. When you connect to higher realms, you're handing over whatever you are holding onto, for example, your fears and worries. Meditation is a wonderful way to practice this. As you move along in this journey, you may also notice subtle changes in yourself. Maybe you don't necessarily see anything during meditation, but afterward you notice you are being a little kinder and gentler to yourself. Or you feel stronger, more able to set limits and boundaries. These are all signs your spiritual team has heard you and that you are in fact benefiting from this practice.

MEDITATION STYLES

Some of the greatest teachers and ascended beings of all time, like Buddha, remind us how meditation can reduce states of attachment and increase compassion. As the Buddha said, "Attachment is the state of suffering." Through meditation I have found myself letting go of taking on too many tasks or needing things to be perfect. Getting to know different meditation styles can help; following are different styles to play with. I encourage you to give them all a try and see which works best with your learning style. For example, if you are more of a visual learner, then you may do better with guided visualizations. If you're more hands-on, you may find meditation techniques such as mandala coloring to be beneficial. If you're a feeler or an empath, you may enjoy meditations that are heart centered, like the focused meditation or loving kindness meditation below.

These types of meditation have been extensively researched by scientists: mantra meditation, mindfulness-based stress reduction, loving kindness meditation, focused meditation, and mandala meditation. Let's take a moment to get to know each one now.

Mantra Meditation

This is when you mentally repeat a word or phrase until you reach a state of inner peace. It can be a word like peace, love, or *so hum,* which in Sanskrit means "I am one with the universe." When you repeat the word dozens of times out loud, this can be considered a form of chanting.

In Part 3, you will learn the seed sound mantras, which correspond with each chakra. You can also take your mantra practice a bit further and practice with a certified teacher. I personally tend to favor this type of meditation; one of my practices includes repeating a mantra such as *Sa,* which is Sanskrit for infinity. If you want to learn more about mantras themselves, you can check out my book *Mantras Made Easy.*

I have also used the name of Spirit guides and archangels (as you will have a chance to) like a mantra. For example, you could repeat the name of the guide as you hold a pair of mala beads. Mala beads are designed for the purpose of meditation. A mala has 108 beads, and the idea is you recite a word, phrase, or sound out loud 108 times in a row as you move along each bead.

According to the National Library of Medicine, mantras are a great tool to help improve attention and emotional regulation. Repeating a word, syllable, or phrase out loud dozens of times can be considered a form of chanting. Research has shown many positive effects from this practice, including the potential to improve the functioning of your brain and reduce cognitive decline.

In Part 3 you'll learn seed sound mantras (short sounds, some-times called bija mantras) that correspond with each chakra.

Mindfulness-Based Stress Reduction (MBSR)

This is a rather newer style of meditation developed by Jon Kabat-Zinn in 1979 to help with chronic pain and mental health conditions, and is taught by individuals trained in this type of meditation-based therapy. Mindfulness-Based Stress Reduc-tion (MBSR) is a blend of mindfulness and yoga. It teaches you to focus on your breath moving in and out of your lungs, or using your awareness to do a body scan. For example, start at the crown of your head while sitting or lying down, and scan your body gently with your awareness. Give yourself permission to pause and observe when you notice an area of tightness and tension. By resting your awareness on that area and focusing on your breathing, give that area of your body permission to let go and relax. There's a ton of research online that shows this type of meditation reduces symptoms of stress, anxiety, and depression, and can assist with emotional regulation and social anxiety disorders.

One way to apply this technique to your *Just Ask Spirit* practice is to visualize a ray of light (such as the white ray of light) moving in and out of your lungs, circulating throughout your entire body as you breathe. Or perhaps you associate one of your guides with a different ray of light, such as pink or blue. Practice visualizing the colors as you breathe in and out through your nose.

Loving-Kindness Meditation

Loving-kindness meditation (also known as metta loving-kindness) is a type of meditation offered in the Mindfulness-Based Stress Reduction training developed by Jon Kabat-Zinn. Research shows that loving-kindness meditation significantly reduces symptoms in individuals diagnosed with post-traumatic stress disorder (PTSD), trauma, schizophrenia, people suffering with loneliness, and more (National Library of Medicine). "The rationale for the practice is that generating goodwill toward all living beings banishes fear because loving-kindness and fear cannot coexist. Metta is protective, both physically and mentally" (Ñanamoli Thera, 1994).

Here's how to do a loving-kindness meditation after your Cleanse:

Position your body in a comfortable seated position.

Draw your attention inward by closing your eyes.

Think of someone who loves you very much.

This could be someone from the past, present, living, or in Spirit.

Repeat this phrase:

May you live with ease, may you be happy, may you be safe and healthy.

Now repeat this phrase, only this time focus on someone more neutral, like a neighbor.

May you live with ease, may you be happy, may you be safe and healthy.

The third time will be toward someone you don't get along with.

May you live with ease, may you be happy, may you be safe and healthy.

Then extend this wish to all beings on the fourth round.

May you live with ease, may you be happy, may you be safe and healthy.

Finally, you may include yourself.

May I live with ease, may I be happy, may I be safe and healthy.

Consider calling in one of your Spirit guides to be with you as you practice this meditation.

Focused Meditation

Focused meditation includes concentrating on one thing at a time using your five senses. Examples of focused meditation include counting mala beads, listening to the sound of a singing bowl, counting your breath (*inhale . . . one . . . two . . . three . . . exhale . . . etc.*), candle gazing, and chakra meditation. Long-term studies reported by the National Library of Medicine illustrate promising feedback for using meditation as a way to prevent Alzheimer's disease and in the rewiring of the neural networks in the areas of the brain involving memory. Since focused meditation can be done in just a few minutes, this may be an ideal form of meditation to practice as you focus on one of your spiritual team members in Part 3.

For example, you may invoke an ascended being or archangel by clanging the sound of a bell or Tibetan bowl and then focus on the sound as you feel and sense your Spirit guides around you.

Mandala Meditation

My mother-in-law is a devout Catholic. For years she used to get on me for taking my children to an Episcopal church. Each time we'd get together, she would somehow manage to make a comment (which at the time felt like a jab) about the fact that my children were not confirmed in the Catholic Church. She knew I was into yoga, meditation, and all sorts of other stuff and saw these practices as moving away from the church rather than as a means for becoming closer to God. Then one day, I received a text with a picture of monks at a local college in her area. They had come into town for the weekend, and since it was a Catholic college, she decided to attend the event. She bought me a blanket the monks had made; I still use it today when I do energy healing on a client. I'm not sure what happened that weekend, but being around those monks making sand mandala art gave her a change of heart. From that point forward, she never brought the subject up again.

The word *mandala* is Sanskrit for circle. The creation of sand mandalas, where millions of grains of colored sand are arranged in geometric designs or patterns, is a sacred ritual of Buddhist art used to focus your attention. This form of art is said to evoke higher states of consciousness that help you evolve spiritually. There are many studies on the benefits of mandala coloring, including this one put out by the National Library of Medicine in which a positive correlation between mandala coloring, mindfulness, and overall well-being in terms of creating positive emotions was found.

You can easily find black-and-white mandalas for you to trace, draw, copy, or color online or in local shops where books are sold. You may also draw your own shapes as you connect to Spirit on a blank piece of paper. I call this *autonomic coloring* and discuss this later. Keep in mind each mandala corresponds to your chakras; therefore, as you color, trace, or draw, this can be a fun, creative way to develop your channeling abilities.

Now that you have had a chance to look over different styles of meditation, let's take a moment to practice. Following is a Crown Chakra Meditation I encourage you to listen to (if you are listening to the audiobook) or read through slowly. Notice when you are done any sensations you feel in your crown chakra area.

Crown Chakra Meditation

Take a moment to sit up nice and tall in a comfortable seated position. Relax your shoulders and place your hands on your lap. Relax. Tune in and notice your breathing. Breathe in and out slowly, counting your breaths: *inhale . . . one . . . two . . . three . . . four, exhale . . . one . . . two . . . three . . . four . . . and inhale . . . four . . . three . . . two . . . one. . . .* Do this two to three more times, inhaling for the count of four and exhaling for the count of four. Pause and with your eyes closed, focus your attention on your crown chakra. The crown chakra is at the top of your head and slightly above it. Since it's close to your brain, it impacts your nervous system. It also represents your connection with your spiritual centers. Keep relaxing your shoulders, neck, and jaw as you connect to this center (again because it is so closely related to the nervous system). You may notice some tension arise in these upper areas; just notice, observe, and breathe gently into any tension.

Now, visualize a beautiful white light illuminating through crown chakra. Picture your crown chakra like a lotus flower, and imagine one thousand petals opening and closing as the energy of the white ray of light moves through you now. Through this divine white light full of purity, harmony, and peace, allow yourself to feel the vibrations the white light carries as you activate your soul star, which is located about a foot above your crown chakra. Allow this activation to reconnect you to your higher self and your divine connection while simultaneously releasing and transmuting any past negative energy or traumas. See this white light radiating through your crown chakra, expanding your consciousness beyond all time, space, and dimension. Relax into this light for a few minutes and then open your eyes, take in the sights and smells around you, and complete your meditation with the same breath pattern: *inhale . . . one . . . two . . . three . . . exhale . . . one . . . two . . . three . . . four. . . .* Place your hands in prayer to close out the practice.

Invoke

You may also invoke one of your team members before entering meditation and ask for specific things like in the examples below:

- Call on Archangel Gabriel and ask for inner strength, effective communication, and higher wisdom. Be sure to say thank you before and after you meditate. Archangel Gabriel will come in right away when you ask. Lean into the vibrations of Archangel Gabriel, and let these higher frequencies run through your body like running water.
- Call on Archangel Raphael and ask him to clear and balance your chakras. Thank you. Meditate. Receive.
- Call on your guardian angel and request clear guidance for your spiritual path and soul purpose. Thank you. Meditate. Receive.
- Call on an ascended being, for example, Jesus, and ask for unconditional love, honesty, and harmony. Thank you. Meditate. Receive.
- Call on the consciousness of Buddha, and ask for forgiveness and compassion. Thank you. Meditate. Receive.

My Spirit Message: Boundaries

I channeled this after meditating with Archangel Gabriel. I had asked for information about how to set boundaries before I went into my focused meditation: direct people back to their strengths.

Here's what I wrote after meditating:

> *When someone is upset or having a hard time you can redirect*
> *them to their own coping skills and strengths by saying things*
> *like "Sounds like this is a really difficult time for you. I am really*
> *glad you have the gym you go to, to help you de-stress and*

*clear your mind." Or "I am so sorry you are going through this,
I bet this is a time when you are glad you have a strong faith
and prayer practice." By redirecting them in this way, it takes the
pressure off you and reminds them of the coping skills they have.
Whenever people go through a hard time, the stress can cause
them to forget or overlook the resources they have.*

CHAPTER 10

EXPANDING CONSCIOUSNESS: MUDRAS

When it comes to channeling Spirit, learning to be present in your body as a resource for regulating the rate, speed, and circulation of energy is essential.

When a woman named Clare was struggling to sit still while breathing in my yoga class, I suggested she put her hands in a *mudra*. She had come up to me beforehand to let me know she had vertigo and would therefore need to adapt some poses. When I saw her rubbing her neck and trying to release tension, from across the room

I nonverbally gestured to her to connect her pointer finger to her thumb (like the "okay" gesture) and place her hands on her lap. She did, and I immediately saw her body move into a calmer, less reactive state.

Mudras are sacred hand gestures used in yoga, meditation, and even dance practices. They have been around for thousands of years and can be seen in both Western and Eastern practices. I find them to be incredibly powerful when it comes to steadying your mind, processing your emotions, and connecting to Spirit.

Mudras as a sacred hand gesture alter and increase energy flow (also known as *prana*) between the body and the brain. Having an increased energy flow has a positive impact on your circulation, breathing, nervous system, brain, glands, and muscles. They also aid in the connection to sacred realms.

The word *mudra* in Sanskrit means seal. You are sealing or securing a circuit of energy. Think of it like sealing a pinhole in a tire. Only instead of air, mudras help you both hold and circulate energy so you can access and hold higher states of consciousness more easily. Many ascended beings such as Mother Mary and Buddha have been depicted throughout history with their hands in various mudra postures. Buddha is often depicted with the thumb and index finger together in art and images. Mother Mary is often portrayed with prayer hands, another mudra.

Mudras also help you connect to the five elements: earth, water, fire, air, and space. Ayurveda is one system of medicine that may include mudras as a means to support the treatment of energetic imbalances and stress, which can lead to *dis-ease*.

In Part 3, you will have a chance to get to know fourteen different types of mudras incorporated into the Cleanses provided.

Know each one corresponds to the seven energy centers in your body (chakras). You'll practice holding a mudra throughout during a portion of your Cleanse and, if you choose to, you can take each beyond Cleansing into your meditation or movement practice. As you get to know these hand gestures, you'll see how each finger helps foster your relationship with the elements, and how, when practiced, mudras can assist your emotions in flow. For example:

FINGER POSITIONS
Think of your fingers as electrical circuits that, when you press them together in a certain way during meditation or breathwork, create a channel or loop for the flow of energy. For example, the sun seal mudra can be done by pressing the pad of your thumbs and ring finger together on each hand.

Thumb	Fire, body heat, pure energy Emotions of worry
Index finger	Air, currents of energy in movement Helps with depression, grief
Middle	Space, expansion, anger, frustration
Ring	Earth, bones, organs, grounding, solid Helps with restlessness, distractibility, impulsive behavior Nervous system, emotion of anger
Little	Water, liquid, adaptability Emotion of fear

While there are hundreds of distinct types of mudras, in the Cleanses I selected ones that are simple and easy to remember. With that said, mudras are designed to be held in a certain way to move the energy in a particular way and, depending on the person, some mudras are better than others. Believe it or not, some mudras have contraindications. Therefore, before you take on a mudra practice where you might hold a mudra for an extended period or on a regular basis, it's important to know what they are. Following are the seven main mudras you will be using, the benefits and contraindications, as well as some basic guidelines for how mudras can help you in your practice.

The seven mudras you'll practice in Part 3 are referred to as *hasta mudras*. Hasta mudras are hand gestures that direct the flow of energy to certain parts of your brain and body. It is important to note here, the mudras I share with the Archangel Cleanses do not have contraindications.

HASTA MUDRA

ROOT CHAKRA	
Press the pads of your pinkies together. The rest of your fingers will be folded inward or extended outward. Place your hands on your lap as you hold the mudra.	
Contraindications:	Use caution if you have low blood pressure.
Benefits:	Good for high blood pressure, constipation, cramps. This mudra helps move the energy in your first (root) and second (sacral) chakras, creating a sense of stability, safety, and balance.

SACRAL CHAKRA	
Gently press the pads of your ring fingers together. The other fingers will gently curl inward or extend outward.	
Contraindications:	If you have an upset stomach, use with caution.
Benefits:	Creates a soothing sensation and moves energy in the root chakra and navel area. This can help you develop a sense of trust, confidence, and balance.

SOLAR PLEXUS CHAKRA

Gently press the pads of your middle fingers together. The other fingers will gently curl inward or extend outward.

Contraindications:	Those with anxiety might want to start slowly and gradually work up to longer periods of time holding the mudra.
Benefits:	This mudra helps to detox the liver and kidneys from any stuck or stale energy. This can have an energizing impact on the body, and it helps to boost confidence and personal power.

HEART CHAKRA

Gently press the pads of your index fingers together. The other fingers may be gently curled in or extended outward.

Contraindications:	People with high blood pressure should use caution.
Benefits:	Enhances circulation in the three parts of your lung: lower, middle, upper. Supports breathing and respiratory channels. Activates and moves energy around the heart. Builds resilience and rhythm of energy, purifies energy, and helps support a strong aura.

THROAT CHAKRA

Press the pads of your thumbs together. The other fingers may be gently curled in or extended outward. This mudra activates and opens your throat chakra.

Contraindications:	Hyperthyroidism, breathing problems.
Benefits:	Opens up energy around your throat chakra, enhancing freedom of expression, creativity, and intuition.

THIRD-EYE CHAKRA	
Gently press all the pads of your fingers together, similar to a prayer pose, but the heels of your hands will be separated, creating a dome-like space between your palms. All ten pads of your fingers will be connected.	
Contraindications:	Take it slowly if you have any health conditions.
Benefits:	Opens up all your chakras and helps your emotions flow more easily.

CROWN CHAKRA	
Bend the middle fingers of each hand down to touch the ball of the thumb and then press the thumb gently on top of it to secure the middle finger. Rest the backs of your hands on your thighs.	
Contraindications:	High blood pressure.
Benefits:	Activates and energizes the upper chakras including the crown chakra. This mudra has purifying effects on the body, helping you open up to the spaciousness of energy and the Divine.

BASIC GUIDELINES FOR PRACTICING MUDRAS

I recommend that you hold each mudra for a minimum of one to two minutes. To get the full benefits of a mudra you can hold them longer—even forty-five minutes to one hour. This is why they are ideal for meditation practices. With that said, since a mudra is the second step of the Cleanse (Look Inward) I encourage you to hold it (taking them apart, as needed, to write down Spirit messages or observations in your notebook), as you move through all seven steps. This will get you in the habit of holding a mudra for a few minutes each day. If you are in elevated levels of reactivity (high stress), as long as there are no contraindications, you may move through a Cleanse twice a day, morning and evening, holding a mudra.

Worth noting is how mudras can influence your breathing. I remember moving through a Cleanse, and then asking the archangels and ascended beings to come in and assist me in the writing of this book. I spoke these words out loud: "Show me, guide me, teach me how to guide others to connect to the light of Spirit." As I spoke these words, I felt an incredibly grounding sensation. Whenever I feel a strong presence, I sense the energy of an ascended being coming in. Sometimes I hear their name, or see a color or an image. The energy was so strong, the rhythm of my breath became slow and deep. In my mind, I thought, *I better get writing; my family members will be up soon.* (I always write when everyone is asleep.) But instead, I was guided to connect all ten fingers into a mudra similar to prayer, with only the heels of my hands open like a dome. Placing my hands into this mudra allowed me to remain calm and sit a while longer so I could fully take in the force of energy that was moving through me. What I learned was that sometimes the energy of an ascended being comes in so strong, it can cause you to temporarily react, like I did. Whenever your thoughts come in quickly and have a rushed or panicky tone, these can be signs of triggers, that is, energy moving, releasing. Mudras can help you move through them.

I imagine that is what the ascended beings did when they were practicing and learning these spiritual tools. Like us, they too had to learn how to harness the energy of Spirit, so they could move beyond thinking into states of calm and bliss. Learning to master the power of your own breath will also help.

My Spirit Message: Insights on the Unexpected

In Spirit there are no surprises. I received this message after a dear friend's mother had passed. The passing was unexpected, and when I spoke to my friend she was in shock.

In Spirit there are no surprises.

I turned to Spirit for support, and I heard these two words as I sat in meditation: *still waters.* Then Spirit went on to tell me, *In Spirit there are no surprises.* I later told my friend about the message, and she said it brought her relief.

CHAPTER 11

THE SOUND OF SPIRIT: MANTRAS

*Ruminating is a form of
misusing the element of space.*

Energy and vibration promote healing, connection, and energetic flow through the power of sound. This chapter takes you a bit further into the world of mantras synthesized with the practice of chanting, which has been practiced by meditators and in religious ceremonies throughout history. As mentioned earlier, mantras, when repeated, help free your mind from things like judgments, expectations, and daily pressures. As the energy of these attachments is released, your vibration increases, thus opening you up to receive guidance from your spiritual team.

Studies like this one in the blog Medium.com show that "Gregorian chants (which are part of the Roman Catholic tradition) can help us tune our brains into the alpha waves by enabling us to focus on the structure of the rhythms without even knowing it. The chants can help us to increase awareness, set goals, improve a skill and understand our life's purpose."

I often play mantras in the background of my day, to relax my body and tune into Spirit. You can find a variety of artists who integrate mantras into their music on YouTube and other streaming platforms. Scholars believe, in India, mantras were first used in 1000 BC, while some suggest that mantras predate language. In 2017, I published a book called *Mantras Made Easy*. At the time of writing that book, I had three solid mantra practices. Since then, they've become one of my most frequent go-to spiritual tools for emotional resiliency. In my opinion, the Spirit energy of mantras helps me move toward rather than away from love even in the most troubling and complicated times.

WHAT IS A MANTRA?

A mantra is a sound, syllable, or phrase that is repeated as a chant. The difference between a mantra and an affirmation is in both the technique and the history. In the West, affirmations were popularized in the 1990s by self-help authors such as Louise Hay. Mantras go back thousands of years and are typically repeated out loud as a form of a meditation practice. Therefore, a mantra practice can last several minutes, whereas an affirmation you might repeat only a handful of times.

When it comes to curating your own spiritual practice, you may

turn to both mantras and affirmations. Since both are rooted in intention and in the now, they can be a way for you to evoke and connect to the energy of Spirit. A simple sound such as *ahh . . . aum . . .*
or *om* (which is said to be the sound of creation) can be a wonderful
way to tend to your heart, liven your third eye (both are perception
centers), and fortify inner strength. If you prefer a mantra closer to
what you experience in religious ceremonies, the word *aen* or Jesus's
name in Hebrew, *Yeshua*, can also be repeated out loud.

If you're musical or drawn to music, it can be fun to strike a chord
or play around on a piano while working with mantras. I have a har-
monium, which is like a small organ. I took lessons just so I could
have enough information about how to pair the sounds with music.
For whatever reason, I took a break and stopped playing for a time.
Then I went to see a Reiki practitioner to receive an energy healing.
She told me after the session that she kept hearing the word *harmo-
nium* as she worked on me. "Does that mean anything to you?" she
asked. I told her I had been playing daily for a while but had stopped.
Her response was "The angels want you to start playing again; they
want to help you but need you to raise your vibration."

The very first song I learned to play was the "Guray Nameh"
chant about bowing to wisdom and receiving protection along your
journey. Within this chant is the sacred sound of *aad,* which means
return to primordial love. When you use this chant, I hope you'll
focus on the meaning: love. This study helped me make sense of it
all, and I hope it helps you too.

> Individuals trained in generating feelings of love and appreci-
> ation while holding a specific intention created a 25 percent
> change in the conformation of DNA. Control groups who were

untrained in Heart coherence were unable to produce an effect despite their intention.

Building heart coherence means learning to work with your breathing as you focus on an intention. It's your intention and attention that direct the flow of energy. As you recite the mantras in Part 3, your intention directs the energy toward toward the consciousness (and vibrational qualities) of the mantra. Essentially, you and the frequency of the energy of the mantras become one.

Once you discover the transformational power of sound and vibration, you may be eager to learn more outside of the Cleanses. A great place to start or to develop is by chanting the seed sound mantras also called *bija* mantras.

As noted by Thomas Ashley-Farrand, "It is possible the seed sounds *bija* mantras were chanted for hundreds of years before they were written down. More information on the history can be found in ancient Hindu scriptures—the *Vedas* and the *Upanishads*. Each seed sound generates a frequency of energy in a specific energy center (chakra). Chanting these sounds can be a means for activating and aligning (balancing) each chakra."

THE *HUM* MANTRA

The mantra *hum* is one I use most frequently while Cleansing, along with an assortment of other mantras. I have taught hundreds of Cleanse practices using the *hum*, yet when I asked Spirit what mantra to include to help transform the energy of fear, I very clearly got the message *Aad*, which is Sanskrit for "to return to primordial love."

When you produce sounds like *hum*, notice how the sound impacts your body. I often notice the way *hum* creates a sensation similar to a massage, producing relaxation. This is because it simultaneously calms your body down, by toning your vagus nerve, one of the largest nerves in the body, which can move you out of fight or flight into states of calm and ease. There are numerous benefits of humming researched and documented, including, the way humming helps you release melatonin (the sleep hormone) and circulate nitric oxide, which supports blood and the reduction of bodily inflammation. Therefore, I encourage you to *hum* away anytime you feel blocked, stressed, or disconnected from yourself and Spirit. Even if you are down in the dumps or overfocusing on things you don't like, mantras are a tool for lifting your energy, breaking the walls of inner resistance, and helping you remove the blinders low energy can often press upon you. When it comes to *aad*, it can feel a bit tricky because of the *D* on the end. Yet I encourage you to concentrate on the *ahh* sound this mantra produces.

CHAKRA MANTRAS: SYLLABLES AND ELEMENTS		
First Root Chakra	*Lam*	Earth
Second Chakra (sacral)	*Vam*	Water
Third Chakra (solar plexus)	*Ram*	Fire
Fourth Chakra (heart)	*Yam*	Air
Fifth Chakra (throat)	*Ham*	Ether
Sixth Chakra (third eye)	*Om*	Light
Seventh Chakra (crown)	*Ah*	Pure

Whether practicing the sacred sounds of *aad* or *hum* during a Cleanse, each practice in this book suggests repeating these sounds three to five times in row. I encourage you to pause briefly in between each one long enough (a few seconds) to receive the vibration. Outside of the Cleanse, if you are looking to significantly raise your vibration and to circulate what is referred to in Chinese medicine as *qi* or *chi* (vital life-force energy), you might want to get a set of mala beads (a type of prayer bead kind of like a rosary) and consider a practice where you chant a seed sound, phrase, or syllable 108 times in a row for ninety days. Some believe this number represents the stages on the human soul's journey; others consider it a sacred number because one stands for God, the Spirit, or your own highest truth, zero represents emptiness and humility, and eight represents timelessness and eternity. Ninety days is how long it takes to establish a habit of energy. Energy can run like a program; if you're not consistent, it will revert to old programming or old subconscious beliefs.

As for me, I have become a little obsessed with mala beads over the years. I keep a set in my car, office, and even wear them as jewelry. My husband, on the other hand, prefers to use a set of rosary beads and tends to turn to prayer while I turn to mantras. There is no right or wrong here, just an open willingness to connect with the Divine.

I mentioned earlier these practices will help you become both more attuned and resilient to energy. What I mean by that is, my husband and I both notice how we are more sensitive to watching disturbing things on television, like violent movies or the news. Yet at the same time, we are more resilient. One of the ways that reveals itself is that we are better able to disconnect from things like television, social media, and negativity itself, put in boundaries, and focus on the things that bring meaning (love) rather than ones that feed ego (fear, negativity).

Whether it's a mantra or prayer, the idea is that you use the beads to keep count. Each time you recite a mantra or prayer out loud, you move your fingers to the next bead until you make it all the way around. Touching each bead along the way is a mindful practice itself, as it helps to slow your thoughts down. Other religions such as Islam also use prayer beads.

USING MANTRAS TO CONNECT WITH YOUR GUIDES

One way to connect with your Spirit guides is to recite and repeat their name out loud, similar to the way you repeat a mantra. It can help to articulate their names by syllables. For example, Ra-pha-el for Archangel Raphael, or Ur-i-el, for Archangel Uriel. You may use Jesus's Hebrew name, Yeshua, which can be easier to chant: Ye-shu-a.

Another powerful tool for connecting to your spiritual team is to use the phrase, "I am." I built this phrase into the Cleanses in Part 3. It can be easy to reference your team as if they are separate from you. This is where the spiritual laws of the universe come in handy. Remember, according to the spiritual law of oneness, there is no separation. Therefore, when you say, "I am," while connected to these higher vibrational states, you are not just *connecting* to your spiritual team; you are *assimilating the qualities of* your team.

This is why I encourage you to be specific about who you connect with. It's like here on earth: When you spend time with a certain group of friends, their habits, beliefs, behaviors, and emotions can be contagious. It's all about intention. If you don't know who you are connecting to, then you may recite the mantra, *I am love* or *I am peace.*

Take a moment now to produce the sound of *aad*. Sit up tall and take an inhale through your nose, inflating your lungs slowly by inflating your lower abdomen. Then, on the exhale, make the sound *aad*. Now, do it again, only this time connect to the *meaning* of *aad* (returning to primordial love) and repeat it out loud with the intention of returning all distorted thoughts or feelings into pure unconditional love.

My Spirit Message: Increase Tolerance for Love

A client once asked if I could help them manifest a new home. They were very unhappy where they lived, as the neighborhood was very noisy. When I asked Spirit what this person needed to do, the message back was increase tolerance for love. Spirit described it like this: sometimes we can have a high tolerance for stress, meaning we become so accustomed to living in disruptive, upsetting environments that we forget what it feels like to be surrounded by love.

In this case, Spirit suggested my client ask Spirit to increase her tolerance to give, to receive, and to remember pure unconditional love.

CHAPTER 12

SPIRIT WALKS: TOUCHING NATURE

When you believe that something didn't work out
as you wanted it to, it might be your soul teaching you
the value of learning to begin again.

It was a beautiful day where I live on Cape Cod, Massachusetts, and I was busier than I thought I would be with clients, but I needed a break. At the time, one of my daughters was homeschooling, and I could tell she needed to get out of the house. Something told me if I asked her to go on a nature walk, she would have said something like "Nah, that's okay." So instead, I suggested we go on a Spirit walk. For whatever reason that day those words intrigued her, and she replied, "Okay."

"Grab a notebook," I said, and off we went to the local café to grab a drink. Around the bend there were some light walking trails and one humongous 150-year-old beech tree.

As we got out of the car, notebooks in hand, I said to her, "If you don't mind, I'm not going to talk." Immediately I saw a little smirk cross her face. I imagine she was thinking, *Yeah, right. We'll see how long this lasts.*

Now picture this, a tree with a canopy sixty feet wide above the trunk and the roots seventy feet wide below the surface. We each found a spot under the tree. I took myself through one of the Cleanses (listed in the 7777 Pathway). When it came time to ask Spirit, I wrote down this declaration (more on this in "Spirit Communication" Chapter 16): *Standing in my divinity as my higher self, I choose to hold the space for love, authenticity, and healing now.* Then I closed my eyes for a few minutes and went into meditation. After ten minutes or so, I took out my notepad and started to write what I was feeling, sensing, and noticing.

This is precisely what a Spirit walk looks like: going out in nature, pausing, moving the energy of your emotions, connecting with Spirit, receiving and recording the information (answers, sensations, feelings, insights, impressions) with whatever comes through. It is all about learning how to harness and hold the space between you and Spirit. As this occurs, you strengthen your states of consciousness. Ordinary sounds, such as birds chirping, become a heightened, savory experience.

GUIDELINES FOR A SPIRIT WALK

SET INTENTION

First thing you want to do is set your intention. Is your intention to go with the flow, tune into the Spirit of nature and see what happens, or are you looking to connect with a specific Spirit guide, a Spirit element, archangel, or ascended being? It's totally up to you.

SILENT LISTENING

While on a nature walk, you might chitchat with a friend, talk out loud about the beauty around you, or listen to music. During a Spirit walk, you pay attention and listen to *energy*. Make it clear to yourself or those around you that a greater part of your walk will be in silence.

EXPLORE WHERE YOU ARE

With a nature walk, you might follow a certain trail and need to pay attention to specific signs, landmarks, sticks, stones, or uneven ground so you don't trip and to be able to get back to where you came from. With a Spirit walk, it's best if you don't wander too far off; instead, explore within the parameters of where you are so you don't have to worry about getting lost. So you might find yourself sitting under different trees, benches, or tuning into Spirit by a body of water.

LOOK FOR HISTORY

It can be fun to explore trails that are near historical landmarks like museums or conservation land. Look for places where Indigenous people lived or where the land is protected from development.

INTENTIONAL PAUSES
With a nature walk, you might find yourself taking breaks for a sip of water or to take in your surroundings. Spirit walks typically have more and/or longer pauses so you can tune in, process your emotions, and jot down messages in your notebook. When you've finished, review your notes by yourself or with a friend.

INDOOR SPIRIT WALKS

When the weather is cold or treacherous you may be less inclined to take a Spirit walk outside. In this case, you can do a Spirit walk indoors. The key is to have an uncluttered space, so you don't trip on anything. You can still invite members of your team (archangels, passed loved ones, guides, ascended beings) to walk with you.

One powerful practice is to ask your Spirit guide to walk counterclockwise with you. In this counterclockwise direction, you may ask them to help you release what is no longer serving you, and then walk counterclockwise slowly and mindfully several times in a row. Then change direction and walk clockwise asking your Spirit guides to increase what you need, such as love, clarity, guidance, direction, protection, or whatever it is you're looking for. Just ask. As you do so, continue to walk slowly and mindfully several times in a row clockwise.

You may want to hold a sacred item such as a candle or crystal when you walk. I like to light my candle as I call in a specific guide such as Archangel Michael, and then walk both ways with the candle lit. Before you blow it out be sure to thank your angels, guides, and ascended beings for walking with you. If you're doing this with children, use battery-operated candles.

LABYRINTH

According to the Labyrinth Society, "A labyrinth is a meandering path, often unicursal, with a singular path leading to a center. They are an ancient archetype dating back four thousand years or more, used symbolically, as a walking meditation, or site of rituals, ceremony among other things. They are tools for personal, psychological and spiritual transformation, to enhance right-brain activity." I lead yearly weekend retreats at the Kripalu Center for Yoga & Health in Stockbridge, Massachusetts. The center has a labyrinth, and I always make time to move through it as a way to center myself throughout the weekend.

Labyrinths can be found all over the world, across many different cultures and religions. If you go to the Labyrinth Society website, they have a locator as well as more information on how they "work." It is said that mindfully walking a labyrinth helps you become closer with Source or God. This could be a fun way to enhance your Spirit walk experience.

My Spirit Message: Triggers Are a Sign of Illusion

Sometimes, triggers are a sign of unhealed parts of yourself; perhaps an emotion that is left unprocessed, while other times, a trigger can be your soul responding to illusion. In other words, you may be turned off by something or someone similar because your soul knows the truth.

CHAPTER 13

SPIRIT WRITING: FEELING AND SCRIBING

*Each time you use the word "when," you are
focusing on endings. If you ask, "What if?" you are focusing
on beginnings. Imagine there are no beginnings and
no endings—then you would have no choice but
to focus on the space in between.*

The act of writing goes back to humankind's most ancient roots—
Mesopotamia (ca 3400–3100 BCE), Egypt (ca 3250 BCE), China
(ca 1200 BCE), and Mesoamerica (before 500 BCE). When it comes
to asking Spirit, trust me, as our ancestors knew, writing is a great
way to develop our skills. Every quote you see at the opening of each

chapter, an epigraph, as well as the Spirit messages at the end were gathered from my Spirit writing. Some came in loud and clear, word for word while others took a little bit longer until I got the gist of the message.

WHAT IS SPIRIT WRITING?

Spirit writing is a type of autonomic writing during which you may not be consciously thinking about what you are writing about; instead you are allowing the words to flow through your hand onto the page. Writing becomes a channel for scribing what you see, sense, feel, and hear psychically. Through Spirit writing channels, psychics and mediums obtain a wealth of information and inspiration from the higher realms.

I often do Spirit writing before I work on a book or as I'm preparing to lead a retreat, to ask questions and receive guidance. Sometimes the guidance is so profound it changes the trajectory of a chapter or module. Other times, I may begin the chapter with Spirit writing, let it flow, retrieve the nuggets within, delete, and rewrite it from the conscious mind.

I also do Spirit writing with clients. They ask a question and then I connect and free flow the answers. You could do this as well. Ask questions and retrieve answers by allowing your pen or pencil to bring through the information. You can also use your computer and type out the responses if that works better for you. I tend to use my computer for longer Spirit writing sessions. Something about keeping the pads of my fingertips connected to the keyboard helps it flow more easily.

How Spirit writing differs from journaling is that it's less directed and self-conscious. This means you're not trying to put your thoughts down together in a composed or structured way. It's perfectly fine and normal for things not to make sense. Think of it like dropping clues on the page. Believe it or not learning how to give Tarot card readings from my friend Anna helped me improve my Spirit writing. This is because I learned not just to interpret the cards by looking at the pictures but also through touch. This can happen with Spirit writing. You can write a word down on a piece of paper and then touch the word with your fingertip to retrieve more information. It's all about energy.

The other difference between Spirit writing and journaling is you're not writing about yourself, your thoughts, feelings, and experiences. Instead, you're a translator for Spirit. Because things like channeling, meditating, and spirit writing can put you in a bit of a daze, you won't be able to always remember what and how you got the information. This is why I tend to go in and out of meditation when I Spirit write. I might jot down some notes, meditate, jot some more notes down, meditate—you get the point.

New to the process? Here are some basic guidelines that can help.

GUIDELINES FOR SPIRIT WRITING

CONNECT TO YOUR HIGHER SELF

Always take the time to connect to your higher self before you begin. This can be as simple as visualizing white light surrounding you or taking three deep breaths. It can help to put calming spa-like (no lyrics) music on in the background, or to sit by a stream of water or under a tree.

FEEL FIRST, THEN WRITE

Increase your vibration by moving into a feeling state. With Spirit writing you don't want to overthink the process. To do this you have several choices. You will see how the first three steps of the Cleanse in Part 3 bring you into a state of feeling calm before you channel information from Spirit. Or you can relax your mind by taking a few gentle stretches, perhaps some neck rolls, or reaching your arms overhead to open up the flow of your energy.

DISCOVER YOUR WAY

Some people prefer to do Spirit writing with pen to paper while others may type on a computer. If you do prefer pen to paper, I recommend that you keep your pen or pencil on the page rather than lift it up and down with your arm, so you don't break the state of channeling as easily.

RELINQUISH EXPECTATIONS

If you're someone who puts a lot of pressure on yourself, Spirit writing can be a wonderful way to teach yourself how to be less judgmental. This is because there is no right or wrong answer with Spirit writing. Instead, you are capturing clues, insights, words, and phrases with zero idea of what they mean at first. Also, every Spirit writing session is unique. Sometimes it flows out in images and then a word while other times you might capture a word before an image. Sometimes you may find yourself making shapes or doodling. My advice is to go with the flow. Trust that the information is looking to come through you and do your best not to think about whether it's right or wrong, connected or disconnected.

GET SPECIFIC

One thing that can help the process of Spirit writing is getting specific about which Spirit you choose to connect with, and the questions you ask. For example, if I'm creating a class on archangels, I specifically call in the archangel about whom I am teaching. I know one of my daughters captured one of our dogs in Spirit by meditating and Spirit writing. You may also choose to focus on an element (like air, water, earth) similar to the Cleanses in Part 3, or the spirit of a flower or bird nearby. It's all energy. Ask yourself, if the spirit of the tree could talk and provide you with answers, healing, and more, what would it say? If you are really having a hard time getting started, consider jotting down some writing prompts ahead of time. For example:

- **Ask your spirit guide to give you guidance about something.** Some examples may be how to set boundaries, or if you're on the right path. Keep in mind, Spirit doesn't really answer yes or no. You'll likely have to learn how to read between the lines.

- **Ask your higher self or guide for information.**
  I call upon _____ to please give me information and guidance around _____.

- **Ask an ascended being for assistance with a loved one.**
  Beloved _____ I call upon you to please share your wisdom, strength, and healing with me now for _____.

JUST SCRIBE!

You may be better at scribing without any specific questions in mind. In this case you would first calm your mind, take some deep breaths, stretch your aura (refer to Chapter 8 for aura breathing) and let the words flow out of you without any need to organize them in a specific way. Sentence structure and punctuation go out the window.

You are just simply connecting and letting it flow. I find when I scribe in this way, it feels more like channeling poetry; I am curious to see if you may feel the same.

My Spirit Message: Healing the Past

To build your inner strength and heal from the past, look at everything as energy. For example, if you were raised by someone who was controlling or critical, then it's likely their own energy centers were not balanced and healthy. When the third eye, for example, has too much energy, this can show itself through symptoms such as aggression, being critical, addictions, being controlling, and/or having a poor ability to set boundaries. Now, if you pair someone, let's say a parent, in that condition (excessive energy in the third eye) with a child who has a slow, sluggish third eye (which can contribute to self-doubt and poor self-esteem), this may contribute to miscommunication, feelings of disconnection, and even power struggles. On the other hand, when even just one person chooses to balance and clear their energy on a regular basis, this can change the relationship dynamic for the better.

CHAPTER 14

EARTHLY ECSTASY: DANCE

*Peaceful relationships are the result
of learning to connect and communicate
from the higher self.*

In *Sweat Your Prayers,* Gabrielle Roth writes: "Our ancestors danced until they disappeared in the dance, till they felt the force of spirit unleashing in their souls."

Dance is a powerful way to be with Spirit. One of my first encounters of earthly ecstasy happened when I was six months pregnant with my third child. Lord knows why I decided that would be an ideal time to get trained as a trance dance facilitator at the lovely

Kripalu Center for Yoga & Health, where I lead annual retreats. While it was a powerful experience, and instructor Shiva Rea was amazing, I don't recommend you try this while pregnant. I spent most of my time seated, propped up against the wall, watching the participants express themselves through a type of communal free-flow dance. When one woman's body started to release the grief, she was carrying over the loss of a loved one, the beautiful memory of Shiva Rea placing her arms around her is viscerally etched into my mind. The feelings of empathy and healing during and within the spaces of the dance were palpable.

Little did I know that a spiritual DJ, who called himself DJ Mantra, was also in that training and that he would later help me co-lead one of my *Just Ask Spirit* retreats. We figured out later that we had crossed paths many times in our spiritual journey, including large community Kirtan's (a call and response singing and chanting style), a true illustration of divine synchronicity. You can find out more about our retreats, which incorporate live music, at sheriannaboyle.com.

Author, Buddhist monk, and peace activist Thich Nhat Hanh famously said, "The next Buddha will be Sangha." *Sangha* in Sanskrit means community. While Spirit walks can be done either solo or with a friend, much of the essence of Spirit dance comes from being in community. We see this illustrated through all sorts of religious group dances around the world: from Sufi whirling dervishes to the Hawaiian hula, from the Native American ghost dance to the Indian Bharatanatyam.

The type of Spirit or ecstasy dance in this book is one that fosters a sense of healing, self-awareness, mind-body connection, self-expression, belonging, and creative exploration. It is a free-flowing unchoreographed movement set within a sacred space with just a little bit of structure to maintain the integrity, intention, and flow of the energy.

It's important to keep the space where you dance open and safe. Just as you wouldn't want someone entering a room during a meditation practice or marching down the aisle during a prayer service, the idea is that the energy of the space is protected. This is why communities of ecstatic dance often encourage three basic rules:

- No talking on the dance floor
- No drugs or alcohol
- No shoes

Some of the elements of Spirit dancing include mind-body techniques such as breathwork, meditation, sound healing (grunting, hooting, clapping are encouraged), visualization, and moving mindfully without restrictions among like-minded souls. Ecstatic dances can be found with a simple Google search. Some are led off with a playlist blending a variety of genres including electronic music while other ecstatic dances have a live DJ.

At first you may find yourself reluctant or ambivalent about taking part in such an activity. Dancing this way may make you feel awkward, uncomfortable, and silly. Yet it's likely the spirit of the group will help you let your guard down just enough to move through the discomfort. The idea is that you begin to dismantle any self-imposed restrictions so you can begin to experience yourself as a liberated being.

If the space is set properly (noncompetitive), the ego (self-consciousness, fear, insecurity) will begin to dissolve. Then you'll be able to move and process your emotions in a whole new way. Soon you will begin to reap the earthly benefits of Spirit dancing.

THE BENEFITS OF ECSTATIC OR SPIRIT DANCING
• Physical movement, aerobic exercise
• Reduces stress, improves mood
• Releases and transforms trauma
• Builds community, sense of belonging
• You can connect to a higher realm, Spirit
• Increases self-esteem and self-acceptance
• Improves your body-mind-Spirit connection

My Spirit Message: Be Like a Tree

A client once asked me about rumination. He said, "I always feel pressured about how much I have to do." I asked him, "Is it about what you have to do, or what you have to deal with?" He responded that it was both. He had to "do" things at work, but he also had to "deal with" things at home. When I asked Spirit about this, I heard, *Be like a tree.*

Spirit explained it this way: when a branch breaks off a tree and falls on the ground, you don't try to repair it. In other words, you don't try to fix, glue, or tie the branch back on. Instead, you let the branch rot and recycle itself into the earth. Humans try to keep too many balls in the air. In other words, they don't let things "die" because they don't fully trust or believe. If someone hurts you, let it go, or if someone is upset, let them be upset. Let things run their course. It is when we interrupt the cycle of life—infinity, life, death, rebirth—that things get overwhelming. Chronic thinking and worrying happens when things, thoughts, fantasies, conversations, dynamics, even dreams are looking to end, yet you won't let them go. Instead, be like a tree.

CHAPTER 15

PSYCHIC ART: CREATING AND EXPRESSING

When you wake up in the morning, ask yourself,
"What do I have to gain?" Maybe it's self-esteem, self-love,
happiness, or connection. Quit focusing on your
losses and become excited about your gains.

Psychic art, also referred to as Spirit art, is when someone receives psychic impressions from Spirit to create images, Spirit portraits, landscapes, and other types of art. Like automatic writing, Spirit art can be described as automatic drawing, sketching, or painting. While many spiritual artists are quite talented, this is not a requirement and shouldn't discourage you from giving it a try. In fact, many psychic artists are either self-taught or have strengthened their abilities by taking mediumship classes. Some of these types of classes and experiences can be found in a spiritualist church atmosphere where mediums are encouraged to draw a deceased loved one in Spirit without any prior knowledge of the person. As you can imagine for the person who lost a loved one, seeing their image sketched onto a blank canvas can be quite therapeutic and healing. Psychics and mediums looking to sharpen their creative skills further may want to consider art or drawing classes.

As with Spirit writing, you're allowing Spirit to communicate through you. If you are not attached to outcome and surrender to the process, you'll be amazed how much this practice can bring you closer to Spirit. It would be through spontaneous coloring on a blank piece of paper that a buried incident would surface in my life.

When I was eight years old, there was a terrible car accident that killed two of my brother's best friends. My brother was the driver; he was just shy of eighteen years old and under the influence of alcohol. At the time, it felt like the entire town was angry at our family. I remember someone rolling down the window in their car and spitting on my mother and me as we walked down the street. It got so bad, we eventually had to move. So, if you are someone who struggles with rejection and shame, believe me, I have been there.

Through Cleansing, connecting, and coloring, I was able to release some of these emotions on paper. I oscillated between closing my eyes, seeing the image, and then translating it to the page. As this occurred, I felt a powerful connection to the ascended beings. The next day, a friend called to tell me she had witnessed another friend talking badly about me. She felt upset about what she heard. I let her know I was aware, and that this had happened before. I said

I just never told her because I didn't want to hurt the relationship between the two of them. Her response was genuine and kind, and it was exactly what I needed in that moment to heal. The conversation reminded me how I felt when I was eight years old. The phone call from my friend brought up the memory just enough so I could process the emotions of sadness and shame.

Here's the thing: your subconscious often speaks in pictures, so art can be a deep and therapeutic way of letting it release. Some may say the two experiences (my autonomic coloring and the phone call) were not related, yet something inside me said they were. Always trust what you feel.

With that said, psychic art is not limited to pencil and paper. You may also capture Spirit art through other creative means such as photography (like shooting cloud formations) and aura graphs (where you might have the silhouette of a body, and psychically draw their aura using colored pencils). The point is, don't limit yourself in the process. See it as an opportunity to strengthen your intuition, and to release what may be interfering with your true purpose.

According to the Neuro-Meditation Institute, when neuroscientists studied the brains of psychic mediums, an unusual blend of brain activity was detected. Some showed slower brain activity in some areas during mediumship sessions while other areas, including the one in the back of the head where visual processing happens, showed elevated brain activity.

When I asked my daughter Megan's art teacher to encourage Megan to sell her art, I was surprised and delighted by her response: "I never encourage people to create art to sell it," she said. "If it comes out the way she hopes and she chooses to sell it, that's fine, but if you go into art painting it for someone else, you will disconnect yourself from the source it is coming from."

In terms of your *Just Ask Spirit* journey, if Spirit art sounds like something you are open to and willing to give a try, a great place to start is to gather some art supplies like a sketchpad, pencils, watercolors, crayons, or pastels. Keep the materials handy, perhaps in a pretty jar or next to the area where you meditate, so you don't have to break your meditative state to retrieve them. As best you can, be consistent about where and when you connect to Spirit. If you return to a space regularly and with the intention to connect, you'll find that as soon as you sit, Spirit will come around.

GUIDELINES TO GET YOU STARTED

Find a quiet location away from distractions, one you can revisit frequently to build consistency.

- Have your instruments (pen, pencils, paper) already available and easily accessible.

- Move through the *Just Ask Spirit* (Cleanse) and when you get to the part where you channel, choose coloring.

- Consider playing some light meditative music in the background. I love anything with *binaural beats* (which create a frequency conducive to relaxation). You can easily find binaural musical beats on YouTube.

- Focus on a specific guide (perhaps your guardian angel) or question as you take two to three deep breaths.

- Let go of all expectations and let Spirit lead the way.

- Ask your questions and/or intentions then through autonomic coloring or Spirit art; allow the answers to flow through you.

- Most importantly, detach from the outcome and enjoy the process.

SAMPLE QUESTIONS
Here are some examples to help get you started: Guardian angel, show me your colors. . . . Higher self, what is my purpose? Can you help me process my emotions around . . . Can you show me my soul's path? Help me to release what no longer serves me. . . .

My Spirit Message: How to Decrease Judgment

When I asked one of my guides about decreasing judgment, I heard, *Treat people as you would a piece of priceless art.* If someone were to show you their art, particularly a child, you would find a way to celebrate the good in it. Apply this to people and situations in your life. Look at them as a piece of art, and do your best to try to view things through the lens from which it was created. Notice the good.

CHAPTER 16

SPIRIT COMMUNICATION

*Vibration is the language of
our emotions.*

Communicating with Spirit can happen both consciously and unconsciously. What I mean by that is Spirit communication can be direct, like a prayer, or indirect through meditation, hypnosis, or trancelike states you might experience in ecstatic dance. Spirit speaks through energy.

Part 3, introduces you to the *Just Ask Spirit* version of the Cleanse. Right around Step 4, activate, I will encourage you to ask Spirit. This is because at this point you are likely out of any fight-or-flight mode and feeling calmer and more relaxed. When I suggest you ask Spirit, there are four ways you do that.

They are:

Intention

Declaration

Prayer

Ask a question

Let's take a moment to get to know each one of them now.

INTENTION

Setting an intention means to direct your attention in a specific way. Intentions can be set verbally through individual words and statements, or nonverbally through visualization or mindful actions such as lighting a candle or incense. In the Cleanse, I encourage you to visualize white light above the crown of your head; this is a form of an intention. You are consciously choosing to connect to Spirit, light, higher self. You are also setting an intention when you show up to your spiritual practice or community. This sends a strong message of discipline, consistency, and devotion.

During the ASK portion of the Cleanse, you may write out an intention. It can be as simple as:

My intention is to gain clarity, or *My intention is to learn, practice, and receive wisdom around letting go.*

DECLARATION

A declaration is a written and/or verbal announcement. It is a statement of where you stand, what you value, and most importantly what you choose. It is a powerful way to utilize your free will.

For example, *I now assert my birthright to claim victory, success,* and happiness. Or *I now claim my birthright to be protected, safe, and free.* Or *Love and freedom preside within me and over me now.*

When you speak or write a declaration, be sure to have a tone of voice that demonstrates you mean business!

PRAYER

Prayer is a way to speak to God and your Spirit guides. It invites God into your life, your situation, and circumstances. Through prayer, you can send your praise and love for your guides by reciting specific prayers, or you can ask for love, support, healing, resolution, and more. A prayer can be a daily devotional practice or an occasional request. It is entirely up to you.

Here is one that I learned from my beloved quantum healing teacher. I memorized and taught it to my daughter Kenzie. She and I recited it nightly together before bed until she was about ten years old. I found this version online:

LORD'S PRAYER, FROM THE ORIGINAL ARAMAIC

O Birther! Father-Mother of the Cosmos
Focus your light within us—make it useful.
Create your reign of unity now—
through our fiery hearts and willing hands
Help us love beyond our ideals
and sprout acts of compassion for all creatures.
Animate the earth within us: we then
feel the Wisdom underneath supporting all.
Untangle the knots within
so that we can mend our hearts' simple ties to each other.

Don't let surface things delude us,

But free us from what holds us back from our true purpose.

Out of you, the astonishing fire,

Returning light and sound to the cosmos.

Amen.

Translation by Neil Douglas-Klotz in *Prayers of the Cosmos*

QUESTIONS

Finally, you can always ask Spirit a question. What I have learned from channeling Spirit is very often you begin with one question and then find ways to narrow it down to something specific. In other words, as you gain information and process emotions, the energy changes; therefore, it is quite common for you to alter or change the question according to what you are seeing, sensing, or feeling. Your question may also be in the form of a request.

Here are fifty-nine ways you can get to know and speak with your guides:

1. What is your name?
2. How will I recognize your energy?
3. Who is my guardian angel?
4. How long have you been with me?
5. What purpose are you aligned with?
6. Tell me more about . . .
7. Show me how to . . .
8. Help me bring forth my ability to . . .
9. Guide me on . . .
10. Give me clarity on . . .
11. What do I need to know about . . .

12. What is in my greatest and highest interest for . . .

13. Tell me more about my purpose.

14. Tell me more about your purpose.

15. How can I improve in . . .

16. Where should I put most of my attention?

17. Dear Spirit, bring forth my abilities to parent with calm and ease.

18. What is the best way to heal . . .

19. Is there anything I can't see?

20. Please send me a mantra or affirmation.

21. How can I support . . .

22. How will I know when it is time to make a change?

23. What is holding me back from succeeding in . . .

24. How do I let go of . . .

25. How do I create more of . . .

26. What is the best way to handle . . .

27. Tell me more about my soul's purpose.

28. How can I increase my vibration around . . .

29. How can I overcome . . .

30. The best way to handle my doubts and fears is . . .

31. How do I love myself?

32. What wisdom do you have for me today?

33. Will this work out for _____?

34. Are my loved ones in Spirit okay?

35. What is the best way for me to get my needs met?

36. Dear Spirit, I ask for your forgiveness around

_____.

37. Do I have everything I need to . . .

38. How can I free myself from . . .

39. What is most important for me to focus on?

40. How can I serve?

41. How will I know you are with me?

42. Please send me a sign.

43. What career path would be best for me?

44. How can I improve my ability to . . .

45. Beloved Spirit, I am open and ready to receive
    _____, thank you.

46. How do I have more _____ in my life?

47. Will things turn out for me?

48. How will I know I have learned a lesson?

49. How can I move on from _____?

50. How can I improve my ability to listen?

51. How can I help myself and/or others feel safe?

52. What are the best ways for me to release stress?

53. What is needed here to increase sales, balance, income, or satisfaction?

54. How do I know when a change needs to be made?

55. What lessons and learnings are required for me to create abundance, balance, and ease?

56. Guide me on how it would be best for me to handle
    _____.

57. Show me what I cannot see in this situation.

58. Highlight the area of my work that I should focus on.

59. How can I create work-life balance?

> ### GETTING TO KNOW YOUR GUIDES
>
> Here are some additional questions to help you get to know your guides. Meditate or scribe to receive answers.
>
> * Beloved Archangel Raphael, please tell me about your staff. How does it help you serve God?
> * Holy Mother Mary, please tell me about your blue cloak.
> * Beloved Archangel Michael, please tell me more about your sword.
> * Ask a loved one in spirit: Please tell me how you are doing?
> * Ask a loved one in spirit: Please tell me who you are with?
> * Beloved Spirit, please send me an affirmation or mantra.

PROTECTION

When it comes to working with Spirit, many people want to know about protection. I want you to know when you hook up to your higher self, you are simultaneously choosing to protect yourself. You will notice in the Cleanse, I always encourage you to connect with your higher self, Spirit, and/or divine white light first (yes, I have got you covered). The remaining steps of the Cleanse are also highly protective. They encourage you to do things like breathe, recite mantras, and tap into your free will via *I am* and *I allow* statements. Each one of these practices by itself raises and nourishes your vibration. When you put them all together the way I have for you in the Cleanse, you are training your energy to be vibrant, resilient, and strong.

Should you feel like you need more protection, I would encourage you to do an expanded form of the Cleanse. The expanded form means you would recite 108 mantras in a row (during the *E* emit, step). One mantra I might suggest is called the Durga mantra. It is for divine protection and removes all negative influences (when repeated 108 times in a row, over a 90-day period). It is: *Om Dum Durgayei Namaha.*

If you would like to take part in my Membership, where you learn and practice mantras, as well as other tools and techniques for taking care of your energy, visit sheriannaboyle.com.

My Spirit Message: Learn to Communicate from the Higher Self

If you are dealing with a difficult person, rather than talk to them directly, connect to your higher self and then call in the consciousness of *their* higher self. *I call upon the higher self of* _____.

Then begin to share your request. For example, *Thank you for treating me with kindness, respect, and compassion.*

CHOOSE:
THE *7777* PATHWAY

*Now that you have the foundation
and tools for feeling and asking Spirit,
it is time to put it all together.*

I call it the 7777 Pathway. The angel number 7777 represents spiritual path, awakening, luck, divine protection, growth, and embarking on a new chapter in your life. When you see it repeated in this way, the angels are amplifying a message of encouragement and trust. While the basic structure is the same as the previous Cleanses discussed in this book, you will notice some slight variations. This is because I am guiding you to process your emotions, connect, and ask Spirit at the same time.

Everything is based on a 7777 framework, yet your actual Cleanse will be 7 steps.

Here is what the framework is based on:

7 Chakras

7 Elements

7 Archangels, and

7 Steps for emotional processing

For the 7777 Pathway, you will need a journal or notebook. If you are someone who enjoys channeling Spirit through coloring or Spirit art, consider a notebook with blank white pages. At the top, cover, or somewhere inside your notebook, write the number 7777 as this can be a great way to set your intention. Before beginning, take a moment to get to know how these Cleanses will work. The basic guidelines are as follows.

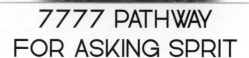

7777 PATHWAY
FOR ASKING SPRIT

Here are the seven steps for asking Spirit:

Step 1. C: Clear Reactivity—Connect to Higher Self

Always be sure to find a quiet location away from distractions. Sit in a comfortable, seated position and begin by choosing to connect to your higher self or, if you prefer, Spirit. To do this, you can visualize white light, a golden ball of light, or the infinity sign (figure eight) above the crown of your head. It helps to take a deep breath while you do this. If you are having trouble sensing or feeling the light, consider stating your intentions out loud, something like: "I choose to connect to my higher self now," or "I choose to connect to divine white light now."

Step 2. L: Look Inward—Repeat and Breathe

Here, you place your hands in a mudra. The purpose of the mudra is to help you circulate and hold energy in your body. Mudras also are a way to keep you feeling calm and balanced as you open up your psychic channels. You can hold the mudra throughout the entire practice or release it in step four when I encourage you to jot a few things down. While holding the mudra, you repeat several stem sentences—a question specific to the Cleanse—out loud or silently. **You will not answer the question** or sentence. Instead, you will respond by taking one inhale (inflate your abdominal area) and an exhale (draw your navel toward your spine). There are between three and four stem sentences to move through.

Step 3. E: Emit—Mantra

Still holding the mudra, you will recite a mantra out loud for a minimum of three to five times in a row for a shorter practice and up to 108 times in a row for a longer practice.

How long you spend is up to you, depending on how much time you are allocating for your *Just Ask Spirit* practice. If you are doing the shorter practice, you might allocate fifteen to twenty minutes. The longer practice takes about thirty to thirty-five minutes. It is entirely up to you. If you are not comfortable with the mantras listed, you can always replace them with the mantra, "hum."

Step 4. A: Activate—Notice, Observe, ASK

Tune into your psychic channels by closing your eyes (if you have not already). At this point, you may release the mudra or continue to hold it. Take a moment to notice and observe the energy within and around you. Keep the things we covered in Chapter 2 in mind (where we covered the psychic senses). Notice things like temperature changes, tingly sensations, vibration, a sense of calm, release of tension, pressure, a heaviness (like a feeling of gravity), colors, shapes, images, and more. There is no right or wrong; just notice without judgment. You may find it helpful to jot a few things down in your notebook as they arise. Try your best not to overthink and to remain in this higher vibrational state. Being in a state of observation means you are ready to ASK Spirit. Your ask may be in the following forms:

- Intention
- Prayer request
- Declaration
- Question

I recommend one ask at a time and writing it down. It is not unusual to change your question during this process. Then allow yourself to naturally move into the next step, and nourish where you will begin to channel and receive information.

Step 5. N: Nourish—Allow and Receive

Now using the modalities we covered in Part 2, you will receive the information through one or two of them. Keeping your notebook handy, jot down what comes through. For example, you may choose to meditate and then jot down what you received. Or you may choose to do one of the breath practices offered in Part 2 and then write what you received. The idea is you get to know which modality works for you. I would encourage you to give them all a try. Don't take the process too seriously—have fun! Feel free to modify the exercises as well. For example, your spirit walk may be a silent walk around your neighborhood, then you return to your notebook and jot down what you received. **The key is to always finish the Cleanse. In words, be sure to complete the last two steps, surrender and ease, to close out your _Just Ask Spirit_ practice.** I encourage you to try one or more of the following modalities as a resource for channeling:

- Meditation

- Breathing
- Automatic writing or journaling
- Automatic coloring
- Spirit walks

Step 6. S: Surrender—I Allow

After jotting down the channelings that came through, turn what you received into an "I allow" statement. For example, if you received an image of a tree and it felt like a message of strength, grounding, or resiliency, then you would state out loud, "I allow strength," "I allow grounding," "I allow resiliency." If you are not sure how to interpret what you are receiving, you may say something like "I allow clarity," "I allow energy," or "I allow healing." Or you may use the "I allow" statements listed for you. Again, no right or wrong here, whatever best resonates for you.

Other examples of how to do this:

If during meditation or while you are doing breathwork, you see yellow light in your mind's eye, your "I allow" might be "I allow yellow light" or "I allow comfort."

If you feel tingly sensations, you might say, "I allow tingly" or "I allow vibration."

Step 7. E: Ease—I Am

Here you will transform your "I allow" statements into "I am" statements. For example, "I allow wisdom" transforms into "I am wisdom." When you repeat these statements, say them out loud. Sometimes your "I allow" and "I am" statements won't match completely, and that is fine. This is what happens when you channel; things change quickly as the information flows in.

Key Points to Remember

- Move through the Cleanse steps in order. Always begin with the *C* and end with the *E* as each step supports the one before it.
- Have a notebook handy.
- Be sure to always finish the Cleanse with the last two steps.
- Be creative and have fun with the process.

In terms of when and how often to Cleanse, that is entirely up to you. Since I use this system to process my emotions, I move through one practice per day. It is also a way for me to nurture my psychic abilities.

Let's begin. . . .

7777 ELEMENTAL PATHWAY

The elemental pathway connects you to seven nature spirits of *earth, water, fire, air, ether,* and *light.* Each element corresponds to the seven chakras.

PRACTICE 1: EARTH SPIRIT

The element of earth corresponds to the root chakra and is often associated with the color red. When the energy (and emotions) in the root chakra are balanced, this helps you gain a sense of stability, grounding, and security. The mantra for the root chakra is the seed sound, *Lam.* When you move through this Cleanse, focus on being open to receiving guidance, clarity, healing, and wisdom from the consciousness of Mother Earth.

Step 1: Clear Reactivity—Connect to Higher Self

Connect to your higher self by visualizing white light or a golden ball of light above the crown of your head. You may also state out loud, "I choose to connect to my higher self now."

Step 2: Look Inward—Repeat and Breathe

Place your hands in a hast mudra for root chakra. Press the pads of your two pinkies together, palms up in your lap. The other fingers will be curled in slightly. Repeat the stem sentences out loud and follow each one with one inhale and an exhale.

Say: *How I feel in my body right now is* . . . inhale . . . exhale . . . (don't answer the question, just breathe), inhale . . . *one* . . . *two* . . . *three* . . . and exhale . . . *one* . . . *two* . . . *three* as you continue to hold the mudra.

Grounding and connecting my higher self now makes me feel . . . inhale . . . *one* . . . *two* . . . *three* . . . exhale . . . *three* . . . *two* . . . *one*. . . .

Connecting to the spirit of Mother Earth Gaia now makes me feel . . . inhale . . . exhale. . . .

Step 3: Emit—Mantra

Sit up tall and take a nice long inhale, and on the exhale, make the sound *lam* three times to five times in a row or more.

Step 4: Activate—Notice, Observe, ASK

Notice any sensations, images, colors, vibrations, or insights that may arrive. Just notice. Feel free to write down anything you notice in your notebook. Now it is time to ASK Spirit. Write down or recite your question out loud.

Step 5: Nourish—Allow and Receive

Now you are ready to channel. Allow and receive messages, healing, or guidance from Spirit through one of the following:

- Meditation
- Breathing
- Automatic writing or journaling
- Automatic coloring
- Spirit walks

_____

_____

_____

_____

_____

_____

Step 6: Surrender—I Allow

Create an "I allow" statement based on what you receive. Or use one provided below. State it out loud.

Say: *I allow grounding, I allow support, or I allow nourishment.*
Write your own "I allow" statement here.

_____.

Step 7: Ease—I Am

Turn your "I allow" statements into "I am" statements. Or use one provided below. State it out loud.

Say: *I am rooted, I am grounded, I am stability, I am resilient*, or *I am unconditional love.*
Write your own I am statement here.

_____.

_____

PRACTICE 2: WATER CLEANSE

The element for the sacral chakra is water. Connect to the Spirit nature of the element water to bring forth the consciousness of creativity, new beginnings, emotional flow, connection, and fertility. The mantra for this chakra is "Vam." Connect to the consciousness of water to process your emotions and to receive healing, clarity, wisdom, and abundance.

Step 1: Clear Reactivity—Connect to Spirit

Visualize golden white light about the crown of your head.

Step 2: Look Inward—Repeat and Breathe

Begin by sitting up tall, making sure your neck and spine are long. Hold your hands in *hasta mudra number two* for the sacral chakra. To do this, place your hands on your lap, palms up, and connect the base of your ring fingers together. The other fingers will be gently curled in or stretched out. Repeat a stem sentence out loud and then follow with the breath. Say: *How I feel in my body right now is* . . . inhale . . . exhale . . . (don't answer the question, just breathe), inhale . . . *one* . . . *two* . . . *three* . . . exhale . . . *one* . . . *two* . . . *three* . . . as you continue to hold the mudra.

Connecting my higher self to my sacral chakra now makes me feel . . . inhale . . . *one* . . . *two* . . . *three* . . . exhale . . . *three* . . . *two* . . . *one* . . .

Tuning into the spirit of water consciousness now makes me feel . . . inhale . . . exhale . . .

Cleansing and processing my emotions in this way makes me feel . . . inhale . . . exhale . . .

Step 3: Emit—Mantra

Sit up tall, take a nice long inhale, and on the exhale make the sound *vamm*. Do this three to five times in a row or more. Move to the next step.

Step 4: Activate—Notice, Observe, ASK

Close your eyes and notice and observe any sensations such as tingling, pressure, light, or calmness. You may even see colors. Now it is time to ask. Ask Spirit via intention, prayer, question (request), or declaration out loud or in writing in your notebook.

Step 5: Nourish—Allow and Receive

Channel the guidance through one or two of the modalities below:

- Meditation
- Breathing
- Automatic writing or journaling
- Automatic coloring
- Spirit walks

_____

_____

_____

_____

_____

_____

_____

_____

_____

Step 6: Surrender—I Allow

Gather the information you received and create an "I allow" statement. You may also use the "I allow" statements below. Recite out loud.

Say: *I allow creativity, I allow clarity, I allow connection, I allow abundance,* or *I allow healing.*

Step 7: Ease—I Am

Transform your "I allow" statements into "I am" statements based on the guidance you received. You may also use some of the examples below.

Say: *I am safe, I am creativity, I am fertility, I am living consciousness,* and *I am deep soul and subconscious healing.*

PRACTICE 3: FIRE CLEANSE

In this Cleanse, you'll connect to the spirit energy of fire. The fire element corresponds to the solar plexus chakra. When this chakra is in balance, it can help you improve your self-esteem, confidence, personal power for positive change, and transformation. Lean into the sacred mantra of "ram" to support your energetic connection.

Step 1: Clear Reactivity—Connect to Spirit

Connect to your higher self by visualizing white light, an infinity sign, a or golden ball of light above the crown of your head.

Step 2: Look Inward—Repeat and Breathe

Place your hands in the *hasta mudra number three* for the solar plexus chakra. To do this, place your hands on your lap, palms up, and connect the base of your middle fingers together. The other fingers will be gently curled in or stretched out. Repeat the following stem sentences out loud and follow each one with the breath.

Say: *How I feel in my body right now is* . . . inhale . . . exhale . . . (don't answer the question, just breathe), inhale . . . *one* . . . *two* . . . *three* . . . exhale . . . *three* . . . *two* . . . *one* . . . as you continue to hold the mudra. *Connecting my higher self to solar plexus chakra now makes me feel* . . . inhale . . . *one* . . . *two* . . . *three* . . . exhale . . . *three* . . . *two* . . . *one* . . .

Tuning in to the transformational energy and spirit of fire now makes me feel . . . inhale . . . exhale. *Now that I am choosing to claim my personal power I feel* . . . inhale . . . exhale . . .

Step 3: Emit—Mantra

Repeat the mantra *ram* three to five times in a row or more. Begin with an inhale and on the exhale recite the mantra *raaammmmm.*

Step 4: Activate—Notice, Observe, ASK

With your eyes closed, notice and observe the sensations, vibrations, temperature, colors, or mental impressions that come through. Ask Spirit.

Step 5: Nourish—Allow and Receive

Continue to channel information by taking part in one or two of the modalities below:

- Breathing
- Meditating
- Spirit writing
- Automatic coloring
- Spirit walk

_____

_____

_____

_____

_____

Step 6: Surrender—I Allow

Based on the information you gathered, create "I allow" statements or recite the ones below out loud.

I allow confidence, I allow personal power, or _I allow positive change._

Step 7: Ease—I Am

Transform your "I allow" statements into "I am" statements or recite the ones below out loud.

I am confidence, I am personal power, or _I am positive change._

PRACTICE 4: AIR CLEANSE

The element associated with the heart chakra is air. Air represents space and the infinite part of you: your soul. The heart is the bridge from the lower chakras to the higher chakras. The mantra for the heart chakra is *yam*. When the heart is in balance, you are able to give and receive love freely. This can offer you peace and contentment. Tune into the spirit of your heart space.

Step 1: Clear Reactivity—Connect to Spirit

Picture a white or golden light above your crown. You may also recite out loud, "I choose to connect to divine white light now."

Step 2: Look Inward

Place your hands in the *hasta mudra number four* for the heart chakra. To do this, place your hands on your lap, palms up, and connect the base of your pointer fingers together. The other fingers will be gently curled in or stretched out.

Repeat and breathe.

Say, *How I feel in my body right now is* . . . inhale . . . exhale . . . (don't answer the question, just breathe), inhale . . . *one* . . . *two* . . . *three* . . . exhale . . . *three* . . . *two* . . . *one* . . . as you continue to hold the mudra.

Connecting my spirit to my heart chakra now makes me feel . . . *inhale* . . . *one* . . . *two* . . . *three* . . . exhale . . . *three* . . . *two* . . . *one* . . .

When I am fully connected to my heart, it makes me feel . . . inhale . . . exhale . . .

When my heart is spacious, open, vibrant, and free, it makes me feel . . . inhale . . . exhale . . .

Step 3: Emit—Mantra

Sit up tall, take a nice long inhale, and on the exhale make the sound *yamm*. Do this three to five times in a row or more.

Step 4: Activate—Notice, Observe, ASK

Notice and observe any impressions you receive (e.g., sensations, colors, changes in temperature).

Ask Spirit your questions, recite a prayer, declaration, or intention. State it out loud or write it down in your notebook.

Step 5: Nourish—Allow and Receive

Channel the information you receive from Spirit by taking part in one or more of the following modalities:

- Breathing
- Meditating
- Spirit writing
- Automatic coloring
- Spirit walk

Step 6: Surrender—I Allow

Based on the information you receive, create an "I allow" statement. You may also use one of the "I allow" statements provided. *I allow healing, I allow balance, I allow receiving,* and *I allow forgiveness.*

Step 7: Ease—I Am

Transform your "I allow" statements into "I am" statements. You may also use the ones listed below. Your statements do not need to match. Just let the information channel through. Say: *I am love, I am compassion, I am forgiveness, I am truth,* or *I am whole.*

PRACTICE 5: ETHER CLEANSE

Ether is the element associated with the throat chakra. Ether has also been referred to as *akasha,* which in Sanskrit means "universal etheric field of which a record of past events are imprinted." The consciousness ether is connected to the throat chakra. When your throat chakra is in balance, you have an easier time speaking, communicating, and expressing your authentic voice. The throat chakra is associated with the color blue and the mantra *ham.* Lean into your authenticity as you connect to the Spirit of this Cleanse.

Step 1: Clear Reactivity—Connect to Spirit

Imagine white or golden light coming through the crown of your head.

Step 2: Look Inward—Repeat and Breathe

Sit up tall, making sure your neck and spine are long. Hold your hands in the *hasta mudra number five* for the throat chakra. To do this, place your hands on your lap, palms up, and connect the base of your thumbs together. The other fingers will be gently curled in or stretched out.

Say: *How I feel in my body right now is* . . . inhale . . . exhale . . . (don't answer the question, just breathe). Inhale . . . *one* . . . *two* . . . *three* . . . exhale . . . *three* . . . *two* . . . *one* . . . as you continue to hold the mudra.

Connecting my higher self to my throat chakra now makes me feel . . . inhale . . . *one* . . . *two* . . . *three* . . . exhale . . . *three* . . . *two* . . . *one* . . .

Connecting to the energy of ether now makes me feel . . . inhale . . . exhale . . .

Purifying and cleansing my throat chakra now makes me feel . . . inhale . . . exhale . . .

Step 3: Emit—Mantra

Repeat the mantra *ham* three to five times in a row or more.

Step 4: Activate—Notice, Observe, ASK

With your eyes closed, observe without judgment. Notice any colors, sensations, temperature changes, a sense of calm, or shifts in energy. Now you are ready to ask Spirit. Write your question, prayers, declarations, or intention statement in your notebook or state it out loud.

Nourish—Allow and Receive

Channel, jotting down notes as needed, using one or more of the following modalities:

- Breathing
- Meditating
- Spirit writing
- Automatic coloring
- Spirit walk

Step 6: Surrender—I Allow

Based on the information you gathered, create your own "I allow" statements in the space provided. You may also use some of the examples below.

Say: *I allow purification, I allow authenticity, I allow truth, I allow soul expression*, and *I allow freedom*.

Step 7: Ease—I Am

Transform your "I allow" statements into "I am" statements either out loud or in writing or use the ones below.

Say: *I am truth, I am self-expression, I am authenticity, I am purification*, or *I am free*.

PRACTICE 6: LIGHT

The sixth chakra (third eye) is represented by the element of light. Light is what enhances your ability to "see" psychically, since this chakra is associated with perceptions, spiritual growth, and wisdom. The mantra for this chakra is *om*. It is often associated with the color of violet. In this Cleanse, you will connect to the spirit of light to gain your insights, wisdom, clarity, healing, and more.

Step 1: Clear Reactivity—Connect to Spirit

Visualize white or golden light above your head. Or state out loud, "I choose to connect to divine light now."

Step 2: Look Inward—Repeat and Breathe

Begin by sitting up tall, making sure your neck and spine are long. Hold your hands in the *hasta mudra number six* for third-eye chakra. To do this, place your hands on your lap, palms up, with the pads of all ten fingers together. The heels of your palms will have space in between them.

Say: *How I feel in my body right now is* . . . inhale . . . exhale . . . (don't answer the question, just breathe), inhale . . . *one* . . . *two* . . . *three* . . . exhale . . . *three* . . . *two* . . . *one* . . . as you continue to hold the mudra.

Connecting my higher self to my third-eye chakra now makes me feel . . . inhale . . . *one* . . . *two* . . . *three* . . . exhale . . . *three* . . . *two* . . . *one* . . .

When I connect to light, it makes me feel . . . inhale . . . exhale . . .

Nurturing my intuitive psychic abilities in this way now makes me feel . . . inhale . . . exhale . . .

Step 3: Emit—Mantra

Repeat the mantra *om* three to five times in a row or more. It sounds like (*Ahhhh ooooooo mmmmmmm*).

Step 4: Activate—Notice, Observe, ASK

With your eyes closed, notice and observe what you see, sense, feel, hear, and even taste. Just notice.

You may even jot a few things down in your notebook. Now you are ready to ask Spirit. Either state out loud or write down your questions, intention statements, prayers, and/or declarations.

Step 5: Nourish—Allow and Receive

Channel the guidance by taking part in one or more of the following modalities.

* Breathing
* Meditating
* Spirit writing
* Automatic coloring
* Spirit walk

Step 6: Surrender—I Allow

Create an "I allow" statement based on what you experienced. Or use one of the "I allow" statements below.

Say: *I allow intuition, I allow psychic abilities, I allow spiritual growth,* or *I allow higher consciousness.*

Step 7: Ease—I Am

Transform your "I allow" statements into "I am" statements either verbally, in your notebook, or both.

You may also use the "I am" statements below.

Say: *I am intuition, I am psychic abilities, I am spiritual growth,* or *I am higher consciousness.*

PRACTICE 7: PURE CONSCIOUSNESS

The crown chakra is connected to the element of pure consciousness. Pure consciousness is wholeness, joy, liberated from the mind. When you are connected to a state of pure consciousness, you are boundless, infinite, and free. Turn to this Cleanse as a way to remember your purpose. Allow the Spirit of consciousness to awaken the deep inner peace within you. The mantra you will use for this Cleanse is *hum*. The crown chakra is affiliated with the color white or gold.

Step 1: Clear Reactivity—Connect to Spirit

Tune into white light above the crown of your head, or state out loud, "I choose to connect to the pure consciousness in me."

Step 2: Look Inward—Repeat and Breathe

Begin by sitting up tall, making sure your neck and spine are long. Hold your hands in the hasta mudra for the crown chakra. To do this, place your palms together in a prayer pose in front of your heart center, keeping the pads of the pinkies and thumbs pressed together, and open up the remaining fingers so it looks like a lotus flower opening (the heels of your hands will be touching).

Say: *How I feel in my body right now is* . . . inhale . . . exhale . . . (don't answer the question, just breathe), inhale . . . *one* . . . *two* . . . *three* . . . exhale . . . *three* . . . *two* . . . *one* . . . as you continue to hold the mudra.

Connecting my higher self to my crown chakra now makes me feel . . . inhale . . . *one* . . . *two* . . . *three* . . . exhale . . . *three* . . . *two* . . . *one* . . .

Evoking the pure consciousness within me now makes me feel . . . inhale . . . exhale . . .

When I am in this state, I feel . . . inhale . . . exhale . . .

Step 3: Emit—Mantra

Sit up tall and take a nice long inhale and on the exhale, make the sound *hum*. Do this three to five times in a row, or more.

Step 4: Activate—Notice, Observe, ASK

With your eyes closed, notice and observe what you see, sense, and feel. Just notice without judgment. Have your notebook handy as now it is time to ask. Tune into the consciousness of Spirit, ask or state anything you like verbally or in writing.

Step 5: Nourish—Allow and Receive

Continue to channel the guidance by taking part in one or more of the following modalities. Jot down anything that comes through in your journal or notepad.

- Breathing
- Meditating
- Spirit writing
- Automatic coloring
- Spirit walk

_____

_____

_____

Step 6: Surrender—I Allow

Create "I allow" statements based on the information that came through or use the "I allow" statements below.

Say: *I allow the infinite, I allow light,* or *I allow pure consciousness.*

Step 7: Ease—I Am

Transform your "I allow" statements into "I am" statements, or use the ones below.

Say: *I am light, I am infinite, I am oneness,* or *I am pure consciousness.*

7777 ARCHANGEL PATHWAY

In this section, you'll find seven Archangel Cleanses. As mentioned earlier, in Chapter 4, each archangel oversees a ray of light. These rays of light have high vibrational energy directly from Source. The archangels also influence and oversee chakras. This pathway differs from the elemental pathway in the hand gestures (mudras) and mantras. When it comes to the mantra, you will be repeating the archangel's name out loud, several times in a row. I encourage you to clap your hands or snap your fingers while you do this. Singing, chanting, and clapping increases your vibration, making it easier for you to connect. The angels love it when you have fun! Once you are done clapping or snapping your fingers, resume the corresponding mudra.

Let's begin.

1 ARCHANGEL ARIEL (ROOT CHAKRA)

Archangel Ariel's name means "Alter" or "The Lion or Lioness of God." Ariel is often depicted with animals, plants, and the elements of nature. If you have questions or requests about how to clear, balance, and protect your environment (perhaps your home or workplace), or to help you cultivate a sense of security and stability for yourself, pets, and loved ones, call upon Archangel Ariel for support.

Step 1: Clear Reactivity—Connect to Spirit

Take a deep breath and connect to your higher self, tuning into light. You may also state an intention: "I choose to connect to the ray of light overseen by Archangel Ariel now."

Step 2: Look Inward—Repeat and Breathe

Place your hands in Prithivi Mudra. Bring the tips of the thumb and ring finger together. The index, middle, and little finger are extended. This mudra helps balance the root chakra.

Say: *How I feel in my body right now is* . . . inhale . . . exhale . . .

Connecting to Archangel Ariel now makes me feel . . . inhale . . . *one* . . . *two* . . . *three* . . . exhale . . . *three* . . . *two* . . . *one* . . .

Connecting to the rays of light now makes me feel . . . inhale . . . exhale . . .

Step 3: Emit—Mantra

Sing or chant Archangel Ariel's name several times in a row. Feel free to clap your hands or snap your fingers while you do this. You may also ring a chime while you do this. Place your hands back in the mudra for Step 4.

Step 4: Activate—Notice, Observe, ASK

Sit quietly, notice, and observe the energy. Use your senses to notice what is happening around you without judgment. Notice how present you are. This is an ideal time to ask. Remember, your ask can be a prayer request, intention statement, declaration, or question. Consider writing it down in your notebook.

Step 5: Nourish—Allow and Receive

Use one of the following modalities below as a means to receive (channel) information from Archangel Ariel. Jot down your impressions (e.g., colors, shapes, sensations) in your notebook.

- Breathing
- Meditating
- Spirit writing
- Automatic coloring
- Spirit walk notes

_____

_____

_____

_____

_____

_____

_____

_____

_____

Step 6: Surrender—I Allow

Take the information you received and turn it into an "I allow" statement and repeat out loud. Or state the ones below out loud.

Say: *I allow strength, I allow balance, I allow nurturing,* or *I allow stability.*

Step 7: Ease—I Am

Turn your "I allow" statements into "I am" statements or recite the ones below out loud.

Say: *I am strength, I am balance, I am nurturing,* or *I am stability.*

2 ARCHANGEL GABRIEL (SACRAL CHAKRA)

Archangel Gabriel's name means "God is my strength." Archangel Gabriel is often depicted with a trumpet, harp, scroll, or white lily. You can call upon Archangel Gabriel when you need support with things like learning, knowledge, writing, communication, speech, creativity, and motivation.

Step 1: Clear Reactivity—Connect to Spirit

Take a moment to connect to the light of Spirit by imagining white light or a golden light above the crown of your head. You may also state your intention out loud: "I choose to connect with the divine light of Archangel Gabriel now."

Step 2: Look Inward—Repeat and Breathe

Place your hands in Kanishtha Sharira Mudra. To do this, place your hands on your waist (as if you have your hands on your hips) just below the ribs with the thumbs at the back of the body and the finger pointing forward. Repeat the statements below and breathe as you hold this mudra.

Say: *How I feel in my body right now is* . . . inhale . . . exhale . . .

Connecting to Archangel Gabriel now makes me feel . . . inhale . . . one . . . two . . . three . . . exhale . . . three . . . two . . . one . . .

Connecting to my sacral chakra now makes me feel . . . inhale . . . exhale . . .

Step 3: Emit—Mantra

Chant or sing Archangel Gabriel's name several times in a row. You may clap or snap as you do this.

Step 4: Activate—Notice, Observe, ASK

Notice and observe through your senses (with your eyes closed, you may resume the mudra here). Take note of what you see, sense, and feel. Now you are ready to ask a question, recite a prayer, or state or write an intention or declaration.

Step 5: Nourish—Allow and Receive

Channel the information (energy) of Spirit wisdom through one of the following modalities:

* Breathing
* Meditating
* Spirit writing
* Automatic coloring
* Spirit walk notes

Step 6: Surrender—I Allow

Based on the information you received, create an "I allow" statement or recite the ones below.

Say: *I allow strength, I allow hope, I allow effectiveness,* or *I allow freedom.*

Step 7: Ease—I Am

Transform your "I allow" statements into "I am" statements or recite the ones below out loud.

Say: *I am strength, I am hope, I am freedom,* or *I am purpose.*

3 ARCHANGEL MICHAEL (SOLAR PLEXUS)

Archangel Michael's name means "like God" or "He who is like God." Archangel Michael carries a sword and is known for his protective qualities. When called upon, he will protect you from negative thoughts or energy. He is also wonderful at helping you develop faith and trust in yourself. He can help you develop self-confidence as he oversees the solar plexus chakra. So, if you are on the fence about anything regarding your abilities, potential, or career, he is a great archangel to call upon, especially if you work in a field that has safety concerns like law enforcement or human services.

Step 1: Clear Reactivity—Connect to Spirit

Visualize a white or golden ray of light above your head. You may also state a declaration such as: "I claim my birthright to divine safety and protection."

Step 2: Look Inward—Repeat and Breathe

Place your hands in Bhudi Mudra. Bring the tops of the thumb and little finger of each hand together. The middle ring and index fingers are extended and separated. Rest your hands on the back of the knees. This mudra assists with balancing the third chakra.

Say: *How I feel in my body right now is* . . . inhale . . . exhale . . .

Connecting with Archangel Michael now makes me feel . . . inhale . . . one . . . two . . . three . . . exhale . . . three . . . two . . . one . . .

When I connect to his mighty sword, it makes me feel . . . inhale . . . exhale . . .

Step 3: Emit—Mantra

Sing, state, or chant Archangel Michael's name several times in a row or more. You may clap or snap while you do this.

Step 4: Activate—Notice, Observe, ASK

Close your eyes, then notice and observe the energy. What does it feel like when Archangel Michael is present? Now is your time to ask a question, recite a prayer, or state an intention or declaration.

Step 5: Nourish—Allow and Receive

Continue to channel information through one or two of the modalities below. Take your time. Jot down your impressions when you are ready.

- Breathing
- Meditating
- Spirit writing
- Automatic coloring
- Spirit walk

Step 6: Surrender—I Allow

Based on what you wrote, create some "I allow" statements. For example, if you felt safe, write "I allow safety." Or recite the "I allow" statements provided below.

Say: *I allow protection, I allow light, I allow truth,* or *I allow clarity.*

Step 7: Ease—I Am

Close out the practice by transforming your "I allow" statements into "I am" statements. Or recite the ones provided below out loud.

Say: *I am protection, I am light,* or *I am unconditional love.*

4 ARCHANGEL RAPHAEL (HEART CHAKRA)

Archangel Raphael's name means "God heals." Archangel Raphael oversees the green ray of light and the heart chakra. With that said, I have found Archangel Raphael can also assist you with clearing and balancing your third-eye chakra. Call upon Archangel Raphael when you are looking for mental, emotional, spiritual, and physical healing. You may also ask for assistance for healing around heartbreak, forgiveness, and betrayal.

Step 1: Clear Reactivity—Connect to Spirit

Visualize white light or golden light above your crown. You may also recite an intention such as: "I am open and willing to receive the divine healing light of Archangel Raphael now."

Step 2: Look Inward—Repeat and Breathe

Place your hands in Kaleswara Mudra. To do this, shape your hand in the form of a heart. The index fingers will be bent inward touching the middle joint. Press the tips of the thumbs together at the bottom (like the shape of heart) and your ring fingers will stretch out and touch at the top. The other fingers will be relaxed. This mudra helps balance the heart chakra.

Say: *How I feel in my body right now is* . . . inhale . . . exhale . . .

Connecting to Archangel Raphael now makes me feel . . . inhale . . . one . . . two . . . three . . . exhale . . . three . . . two . . . one . . .

When I tune into your healing light, it makes me feel . . . inhale . . . exhale . . .

Step 3: Emit—Mantra

Sing, chant, or recite Archangel Raphael's name several times in a row. You may clap or snap at the same time.

Step 4: Activate—Notice, Observe, ASK

Notice and observe any sensations, colors, smells, or vibrations (tingly, grounded, relaxed). Just notice. Now you are ready to ASK. Write your question, intention, declaration, or prayer request in your notebook or state it out loud.

Step 4: Nourish—Allow and Receive

Channel the insights, healing, guidance, clarity, and wisdom through one or two of the following modalities. Jot down your impressions and messages below or in a notebook.

- Breathing
- Meditating
- Spirit writing
- Automatic coloring
- Spirit walk

Step 6: Surrender—I Allow

Create "I allow" statements based on what you received. For example, if you experienced tingly sensations, you may say, "I allow sensations" or "I allow healing." Or recite the statements below.

Say: *I allow healing, I allow love,* or *I allow abundance and freedom.*

Step 7: Ease—I Am

Transform your "I allow" statements into "I am" statements. Or recite the ones out loud below to close out the practice.

Say: *I am healing, I am love,* or *I am balance and abundance.*

5 ARCHANGEL SANDALPHON (THROAT CHAKRA)

Archangel Sandalphon is often referred to as "the angel of prayer" as well as "the angel of music." Archangel Sandalphon is also the angel of earth and creativity. Call upon Sandalphon to assist with sending your earthly prayers and requests to heaven. Sandalphon is described as the twin brother of Archangel Metatron. You can ask Archangel Sandalphon for assistance in sending your prayers and intentions to Source, light.

Step 1: Clear Reactivity—Connect to Spirit

Visualize a white and/or golden light above your head. You may also set an intention: *I choose to connect to the light of Archangel Sandalphon now.*

Step 2: Look Inward—Repeat and Breathe

Place your hands in Anjali Mudra. Place the hands together in front of the heart. Leave a small empty space between the palms (it looks a lot like prayer pose). This mudra helps balance the heart, throat, and third-eye chakra.

Say: *How I feel in my body right now is* . . . inhale . . . exhale . . . (don't answer the question, just breathe) inhale . . . *one* . . . *two* . . . *three* . . . exhale . . . *three* . . . *two* . . . *one* . . .

Connecting to Archangel Sandalphon now makes me feel . . . inhale . . . *one* . . . *two* . . . *three* . . . exhale . . . *three* . . . *two* . . . *one* . . .

Clearing and balancing in my throat chakra now makes me feel . . . inhale . . . exhale . . .

Step 3: Emit—Mantra

Chant or sing Archangel Sandalphon's name out loud several times in a row. You may clap, play an instrument, or ring a chime while you do this; remember, Archangel Sandalphon loves music. Place your hands back in the mudra for meditation and/or breathing.

Step 4: Activate—Notice, Observe, ASK

Pause, close your eyes, and notice and observe sensations, temperature, colors, and vibrations. Now you are ready to ASK.

Write down or state your question, intention, prayer request, or declaration.

Step 5: Nourish—Allow and Receive

Channel the energy, impressions, healing, and guidance from one or two of the following modalities.

* Breathing
* Meditating
* Spirit writing
* Automatic coloring
* Spirit walk notes

_____

_____

_____

_____

_____

Step 6: Surrender—I Allow

Create an "I allow" statement based on the information you gathered. Or recite the "I allow" statements provided below.

Say: *I allow support, I allow divine communication, I allow creativity*, and *I allow love.*

Step 7: Ease—I Am

Transform your "I allow" statement into an "I am" statement. Or recite the ones listed below.

Say: *I am support, I am divine communication, I am creativity*, and *I am loved.*

6 ARCHANGEL URIEL (THIRD EYE)

Archangel Uriel's name means "God is my flame," "God is my light," or "The Light of God." Call upon Archangel Uriel to assist you with your third eye when it feels out of balance. For example, if you feel paranoid, confused, emotionally drained, or anxious, this could be a sign of an imbalanced third eye. Ask Archangel Uriel to assist you in bringing it into balance or make a request that Archangel Uriel only allow positive vibrations in.

Step 1: Clear Reactivity—Connect to Spirit

Visualize a white or golden ray of light above your crown. You may also visualize the white infinity sign.

Step 2: Look Inward—Repeat and Breathe

Place your hands in Padma Mudra. Repeat Anjali Mudra (the previous mudra), only this time open all the fingers (like a flower), keeping only the heel of the hand, pinkie, and thumb together. This helps balance chakras four, five, six, and seven.

Say: *How I feel in my body right now is* . . . inhale . . . exhale . . .
Connecting to Archangel Uriel now makes me feel . . . inhale . . . *one* . . . *two* . . . *three* . . . exhale . . . *three* . . . *two* . . . *one*. . . .
Choosing to clear and balance my third eye in this way now makes me feel . . . inhale . . . *one* . . . *two* . . . *three* . . . exhale . . . *three* . . . *two* . . . *one* . . .

Step 3: Emit—Mantra

Chant, recite, and/or sing Archangel Uriel's name several times in a row or more. If you like, you can clap, snap your fingers, or move your body as you do this.

Step 4: Activate—Notice, Observe, ASK

Notice and observe the energetic frequency of Archangel Uriel. Ask your question and state your intentions, prayer requests, or declarations.

Step 5: Nourish—Allow and Receive

Channel the healing, guidance, wisdom, and clarity Archangel Uriel brings forth through one or more of the following modalities. Jot down what comes through in your notebook or space below.

- Breathing
- Meditating
- Spirit writing
- Automatic coloring
- Spirit walk

_____

_____

_____

_____

_____

_____

_____

Step 6: Surrender—I Allow

Create your "I allow" statements based on the information you receive. Or state the ones provided below out loud.

Say: *I allow personal power, I allow light,* or *I allow truth.*

Step 7: Ease—I Am

Transform your "I allow" statements into "I am" statements or recite the ones below out loud.

Say: *I am light, I am truth, I am confident,* or *I am ease.*

7 ARCHANGEL ZADKIEL (CROWN)

Archangel Zadkiel's name means "Angel of Mercy." Archangel Zadkiel is the angel of righteousness, transmutation, forgiveness, and freedom. Call upon Archangel Zadkiel for emotional healing and to help you remember your divine purpose.

Step 1: Clear Reactivity—Connect to Higher Self

Visualize a white or golden ray of light. You may also state out loud, *I choose to connect to the divine frequency of Archangel Zadkiel now.*

Step 2: Look Inward—Repeat and Breathe

Place your hands in Mandala Mudra. Rest your left cupped hand on your lap, place your right cupped hand on top of the left, and join the tips of the thumbs. This mudra balances all seven chakras.

Say: *How I feel in my body right now is* . . . inhale . . . exhale . . . (don't answer the question, just breathe), inhale . . . *one* . . . *two* . . . *three* . . . exhale . . . *three* . . . *two* . . . *one* . . .

Connecting my higher self to my crown chakra now makes me feel . . . inhale . . . *one* . . . *two* . . . *three* . . . exhale . . . *three* . . . *two* . . . *one* . . .

Tuning into the divine light of Archangel Zadkiel now makes me feel . . . inhale . . . exhale . . .

Step 3: Emit—Mantra

Sing, chant, or recite Archangel Zadkiel's name several times in a row. Feel free to clap your hands or snap your fingers.

Step 4: Activate—Notice, Observe, ASK

Pause, notice and observe any sensations, light, colors, vibrations, images, or impressions. Ask Archangel Zadkiel a question, recite a prayer, intention, or declaration. Write it down in your notebook or state it out loud.

Step 5: Nourish—Allow and Receive

Using one or two of the modalities below, channel the divine guidance, wisdom, healing, and clarity from Archangel Zadkiel. Jot down what you receive in the space provided or in your journal.

- Breathing
- Meditating
- Spirit writing
- Automatic coloring
- Spirit walk

Step 6: Surrender—I Allow

Create your "I allow" statements based on the information you received. Or recite the statements below out loud.

Say: *I allow forgiveness, I allow light,* or *I allow freedom.*

Step 7: Ease—I Am

Transform your "I allow" statements into "I am" statements. Or recite the statements provided below.

Say: *I am light, I am forgiveness,* or *I am free.*

Be sure to take a moment after each Cleanse to offer thanks to your Spirit guides.

AFTERWORD

Dear Reader:

I wanted to take a moment to thank you for allowing me to be a part of your spiritual journey. My hope is that you've come to recognize your emotions as the Spirit within. Through these practices I am confident you are well on your way to discovering purpose. Most of all, my hope is you are able to see and feel how much you are loved.

You may be wondering where you go from here. All I can say is continue to meditate, breathe, chant, color, dance, dream, wonder, evolve, speak, sing, Cleanse, ask, claim, listen, receive, give thanks, and expand. Carry on, my friend, and I do hope our souls meet again.

Much love,
Sherianna

OTHER BOOKS
BY SHERIANNA BOYLE

Energy in Action: A Book About the Spiritual Laws of the Universe
Emotional Detox Now: 135 Self-Guided Practices to Renew Your
Mind, Heart and Spirit
Emotional Detox for Anxiety
Emotional Detox: 7 Steps to Release Toxicity and Energize Ease
Mantras Made Easy
The Four Gifts of Anxiety
Choosing Love
The Conscious Parenting Guide to Childhood Anxiety
Everything There Is to Know About Childhood Anxiety
Powered by Me for Educators

RESOURCES

FREE RESOURCES

Chakra and mandala chart: JustAskSpiritbook.com

Just Ask Spirit free downloadable gift set: JustAskSpiritbook.com

LET'S CONTINUE OUR PATH TOGETHER

Join, Practice, and Learn . . .

The *Just Ask Spirit* Community: sheriannaboyle.com/just-ask-spir-it-community

Attend . . .

A *Just Ask Spirit* Retreat: sheriannaboyle.com/events

Subscribe and Listen . . .

To the *Just Ask Spirit* Podcast: sheriannaboyle.com/podcast

Receive . . .

A *Just Ask Spirit* Session: sheriannaboyle.com/private-sessions

Heal and Grow . . .

With the Divine Healing and Meditation Group: sheriannaboyle.com/membership

Move Your Body . . .

Through Yoga and Fitness with Sherianna: sheriannaboyle.com/yoga-membership

Visit . . .

The *Just Ask Spirit* Marketplace: sheriannaboyle.com/marketplace

ACKNOWLEDGMENTS

To Alice Peck, my editor. This is our fifth book together. For your talent, guidance, and unwavering love and commitment to the work we create. To Steve Harris, my literary agent, for believing in me and my work. To Health Communications, Inc., the publisher of this book, and their team: thank you for your enthusiasm, guidance, and support. A special shout out to Larissa who designed the cover and interior of this book; you are amazing! Thank you to Christine and Lindsey for all your hard work and kind hearts. To my team, Jason Peterson and Christine Darby, for your wisdom, patience, loyalty, and talents. To my mother, Judy, for your unconditional love and for encouraging me to write this book. To Makenzie, my third daughter and spirit walk companion, for your kind nature and loving soul. To Megan, for the laughter you give me and for the spirit of your intelligence. To Mikayla, for eagerly assisting at the spiritual retreats, your psychic spirit, and wisdom. To my husband, partner, and best friend, Kiernan—words could never describe the love I have for you. To the members of my community, for giving me the privilege to be your guide. To Bonne Blue, for your lovely Reiki sessions and for teaching me the archangel song. Finally, I'd like to give a special and heartfelt thank-you to Spirit.

REFERENCES

CHAPTER 1

Bailey, Alice A. *Esoteric Psychology.* Lucis Trust. 1936. pp. 109, 130.

Practicing a Course in Miracles: A Translation of the Workbook in plain language, with mentor's notes. O Books is an imprint of John Hunt, Publishing. 2011 pp. 352, 353.

Hawkins, David R., M.D., Ph.D. *Power vs. Force: The Hidden Determinants of Human Behavior.* Hay House Publishing, 2012 pp. 90, 91.

Myss, Caroline. *Anatomy of the Spirit: The Seven Stages of Power and Healing.* Harmony Books. 1996. pp. 68.

Tolle, Eckhart. "Realizing the 'Deep I.'" Eckhart Tolle, Official Site - Spiritual Teachings and Tools for Personal Growth and Happiness, May 1, 2023. https://eckharttolle.com/realizing-the-deep-i/.

Cannon, Dolores. *The Convoluted Universe,* Series. Ozark Mountain Publishing. 2001.

Weiss, Brian L. MD. Many Lives, Many Masters. Fireside Publishing. 1988.

CHAPTER 2

National Library of Medicine. "Neuropeptides and inflammation." https://www.ncbi.nlm.nih.gov/pmc/articles/PMC5244030/.

National Library of Medicine. "Neuropeptides and cellular turnover." https://www.ncbi.nlm.nih.gov/pmc/articles/PMC5424629/.

National Library of Medicine. Neuropeptides help to awaken the senses." https://www.ncbi.nlm.nih.gov/pmc/articles/PMC5424629/.

American Psychological Association "Emotions are conscious mental reactions (such as anger or fear) usually directed toward a specific object and typically accompanied by physiological and behavioral changes in the body." Adapted from Merriam-Webster https://www.apa.org/topics/emotions.

Pert, Candace B. Ph.D. *Molecules of Emotion: The Science Behind Mind-Body Medicine.* Scribner Publishing, 2003. Pp. 189, 190.

Pert, Candace B. Ph.D. "The Wisdom of the Receptors: Neuropeptides, the emotions and bodymind." American Psychological Association. APA PsycNet. https://psycnet.apa.org/record/1988-03622-001D.

Tarrant, Jeff. *Becoming Psychic: Lessons from the Minds of Mediums, Healers and Psychics.* Heal Communications, Inc. 2023. https://www.neuromeditationinstitute.com/listedproviders/jeff-tarrant.

Taylor, Jill Bolte, Ph.D. *My Stroke of Insight:* A Brain Scientists Personal Journey. Penguin Books. 2009. p. 65.

CHAPTER 3

Easwaran, Eknath. *The Dhammapada.* Nilgiri Press. The Blue Mountain Center Meditation. 2007. pp. 82.

Wahbeh ND, M.C.R. *The Science of Channeling: Why You Should Trust Your Intuition & Embrace the Force that Connects Us All*. New Harbinger Publications. 2021. pp.97, pp. 119.

McTaggert, Lynn. "The Intention Experiment, The Power of Eight." *Just Ask Spirit* podcast. Dec 17, 2023. https://www.podbean.com/ew/pb-9yyq4-152a015

Sharma, Lakshmi. The meaning of the mantra "Aad" Yoga. https://poseurs.us/aad-guray-nameh-meaning/

The Kybalion: Chapter XII. Causation. (n.d.). Accessed April 27, 2024. https://sacred-texts.com/eso/kyb/kyb14.htm#:~:text=The%20Teachings%20are%20that%20a,which%20the%20matter%20is%20examined

"Bio-Field and Aura." Institute of Biodynamic Medicine, December 18, 2023. https://biodynamic.org/what-is/bio-field-and-aura/.

Myss, Caroline, PhD. *The Anatomy of the Spirit: The Seven Stages of Power and Healing*. Penguin Random. 1996.

Neuro-Linguistic Programming (NLP) Eye movements can show someone is thinking. Excellence Assured. https://excellenceassured.com/nlp-training/nlp-resources/nlp-eye-patterns

Miller, Lisa. Where the Brain Processes Spiritual Experiences. The Journal of Cerebral Cortex. https://news.yale.edu/2018/05/29/where-brain-processes-spiritual-experiences

CHAPTER 4

Bailey, Alice. *Exoteric Psychology 1*. Lucas Trust. 1936. pp. 133.

Choquette, Sonia. Author of *Ask Your Guides*. Beliefnet https://www.beliefnet.com/inspiration/angels/2006/04/get-to-know-your-spirit-guides.aspx.

CHAPTER 5

McClean Hospital. "Understanding Spirituality and Mental Health." August 31, 2023. https://www.mcleanhospital.org/essential /spirituality.

CHAPTER 6

McGreevey, Sue. "Eight Weeks to a Better Brain." *The Harvard Gazette*. January 21, 2011. https://news.harvard.edu/gazette /story/2011/01/eight-weeks-to-a-better-brain/.

CHAPTER 7

Brown, Brené. "Listening to Shame." Ted Talk. March 2012. https:/ /youtu.be/L0ifUM1DYKg.

Walters, Meg. "Healing Crystals What They Can and Can't Do." Healthline. July 20, 2023. https://www.healthline.com/health/healing -crystals-what-they-can-do-and-what-they-cant.

CHAPTER 8

Halpern, Marc, Dr. Ayurveda College. July 1, 2017. https:/ /www.ayurvedacollege.com/blog/ayurveda-and-subtle-astral-body -anatomy-72000-nadis-subtle-body/.

Park, Tosca. "Yoga Basics. The definition of Samskaras." May 2, 2022. https://www.yogabasics.com/connect/yoga-blog/samskaras -unraveling-the-conditioned-self/.

Lloyd, Deborah. "Archangels and the Chakras pdf." Author of *22 Messages from the Archangels*. Create Space Independent Publishing Platform. 2017. https://reikirays.com/wp-content/uploads/2017/12 /Archangels-and-the-Chakras.pdf.

CHAPTER 9

National Library of Medicine. "Effectiveness of Mantra-Based Meditation on Mental Health: A Systematic Review and Meta-Analysis." March 13, 2022. https://www.ncbi.nlm.nih.gov/pmc/articles/PMC8949812/.

National Library of Medicine. "Mindfulness Meditation Is Related to Long-Lasting Changes in Hippocampal Functional Topology during Resting State: A Magnetoencephalography Study." Dec 18, 2018. https//www.ncbi.nlm.nih.gov/pmc/articles/PMC6312586/.

CHAPTER 11

Earth Chant Day. "Tuning Your Brain to Alpha Waves with Gregorian Chant." October 19, 2018, Medium.com. https://medium.com/@earthchantday/tuning-your-brain-to-alpha-waves-with-gregorian-chant-abaa7150c1d7#:~:text=Gregorian%20chants%20can%20help%20us,and%20understand%20our%20life's%20purpose.

Transcendental Meditation. "What Is Transcendental Meditation?" Accessed April 27, 2024. https://www.tm.org/transcendental-meditation.

Burgin, Timothy. "Bija Mantras: Definition, Types and Benefits." Yoga Basics Newsletter, October 13, 2022. https://www.yogabasics.com/connect/yoga-blog/bija-mantras/.

Ashley-Farrand, Thomas. *Healing Mantras: Using Sound Affirmations for Personal Power, Creativity, and Healing.* New York, NY: Wellspring/Ballantine, 2008.

CHAPTER 12

The Labyrinth Society. "Learn about Labyrinths." Accessed April 27, 2024. https://labyrinthsociety.org/about-labyrinths.

CHAPTER 14

Roth, Gabrielle. *Sweat Your Prayers: The Five Rhythms of the Soul Movement as Spiritual Practice*. Tarcher Perigg Publishing. 1998. pp.6.

Marz, Mario. Also known as DJ Mantra. Mariomarz.com, djmatraji.com

CHAPTER 15

Blog, "The Mind of the Medium: The Art and Science of Psychic Mediumship." NeuroMeditation Institute, Eugene, OR. June 5, 2020.

MacKian, Sara. "Spirit Art: Mediumship, Art and the Unseen Landscapes of Spirit..." Everyday Spirituality. Accessed April 27, 2024. https://www.open.ac.uk/blogs/EverydaySpirituality/?p=330#:~:text=%E2%80%9CSpirit%20art%20is%20the%20drawing,art%20rather%20than%20spoken%20language%E2%80%A6.

CHAPTER 16

The Aramaic New Testament. Lord's Prayer. http://aramaicnt.org /2007/06/09/o-father-mother-birther-of-the-cosmos/.

PART 3

The Heart Center. https://www.heartscenter.org/Teachings/WisdomTeachings/ArchangelsandArcheiai/tabid/458/Default.aspx.

Professional Yoga Therapist Manual. Volume 1: Foundations. Integrative Yoga Therapy. Information on Mudras. Le Page, Joseph. 2007.

Akbari, Mehdi, and Hossaini, Sayed Morteza. "The Relationship of Spiritual Health with Quality of Life, Mental Health, and Burnout: The Mediating Role of Emotional Regulation." PubMed Central (PMC). Accessed April 27, 2024. https://www.ncbi.nlm.nih

.gov/pmc/articles/PMC5994229/#:~:text=Their%20researches%20
have%20shown%20that,and%20no%20stress%20(36.

Liu, Chao, Hao Chen, Chia-Yi Liu, Rung-Tai Lin, et al. "Coop-
erative and Individual Mandala Drawing Have Different Effects on
Mindfulness, Spirituality, and Subjective Well-Being." *Frontiers in
Psychology*, October 9, 2020. https://www.ncbi.nlm.nih.gov/pmc
/articles/PMC7581735/.

Raghuram, Y. S. and Dr. Masana, M.D. "Anjali Mudra – Meaning,
Procedure, Benefits, Tridosha Effect." EasyAyurveda.com, December
10, 2019. https://www.easyayurveda.com/2019/12/10/anjali-mudra/.

ELEMENTAL PATHWAY

"Masaru Emoto." Wikipedia. Accessed April 27, 2024. https:/
/en.wikipedia.org/wiki/Masaru_Emoto.

"Air (classical Element)." Wikipedia. Accessed April 27, 2024.
https://en.wikipedia.org/wiki/Air_(classical_element).

"Aether_(classical_element)." Chemeurope.com. Accessed April
27, 2024. https://www.chemeurope.com/en/encyclopedia/Aether
_(classical_element).html.

Baker, Daniel. "Are We Body-and-Soul or Body-Soul-and-
Spirit?" Cornerstone Fellowship Church of Apex. Accessed April 27,
2024. https://cornerstoneapex.org/blog/are-we-body-and-soul-or
-body-soul-and-spirit#:~:text=He%20doesn't%20mean%20that
,distinction%20between%20soul%20and%20spirit.

Church, Dawson. *Genie in Your Genes*. Carlsbad, CA. Energy
Psychology Press, 2018.

Clarity Center. "Chakras & the Angelics (and Science!)." Clarity
Center, April 9, 2024. https://www.myclaritycenter.com/post/chakras
-the-archangels-and-science.

Colino, Stacy. "Why Decluttering Is Important for Self-Care and Wellness." Accessed April 27, 2024. https://www.everydayhealth.com/healthy-living/why-decluttering-is-important-for-self-care-and-when-it-isnt/.

Ghaderi, A., Tabatabaei, S. M., Nedjat, S,, Javadi, M., et al. "Explanatory Definition of the Concept of Spiritual Health: A Qualitative Study in Iran." *Journal of Medical Ethics and History of Medicine.* 2018 Apr 9;11:3. PMID: 30258553; PMCID: PMC6150917.

Kerwin Jenkins, Jessica. "Is Humming the New Walking?" Accessed April 27, 2024. https://www.oprahdaily.com/life/health/a45574931/humming-health-benefits/.

Kapoor, Surendra Kapoor. Updated: Apr 21, 2019. "What Is Aura?." *The Times of India.* Accessed April 27, 2024. https://timesofindia.indiatimes.com/astrology/others/what-is-aura/articleshow/68205758.cms.

Menary, K., Collins, P. F., Porter, J. N., Muetzel, R., et al. "Associations between cortical thickness and general intelligence in children, adolescents and young adults." *Intelligence.* 2013 Sep;41(5):597-606. doi: 10.1016/j.intell.2013.07.010. PMID: 24744452; PMCID: PMC3985090. https://www.neuromeditationinstitute.com/listed-news/the-mind-of-the-medium-the-art-and-science-of-psychic-mediumship-2zejw.

Kramer, Adam D. I., Guillory, Jamie E., and Hancock, Jeffrey T. "Experimental Evidence of Massive-Scale Emotional Contagion Through Social Networks." *Proceedings of the National Academy of Sciences.* Accessed April 27, 2024. https://www.pnas.org/doi/10.1073/pnas.1320040111.

Russo, A. F. "Overview of Neuropeptides: Awakening the Senses?" *Headache*. 2017 May;57 Suppl 2(Suppl 2):37-46. doi: 10.1111 /head.13084. PMID: 28485842; PMCID: PMC5424629.

His Holiness the Fourteenth Dalai Lama, Tenzin Gyatso. "What Om Mani Padme Hum Means" Autumn 2002 *Snow Lion Newsletter*, Shambhala Publications. https://www.shambhala.com/snowlion _articles/om-mani-padme-hum-dalai-lama/.

Tibetan Buddhism - University of Hawaii. Accessed April 27, 2024. http://www2.hawaii.edu/~freeman/courses/phil302/13.%20Tibetan %20Buddhism.pdf.

Johson, Jon. "What Is a Qi Deficiency?" *Medical News Today*. Accessed April 27, 2024. https://www.medicalnewstoday.com /articles/321841.

Geno, Rita. "The Meaning of Namaste." March 24, 2024. https://www.yogajournal.com/practice/beginners/the-meaning-of -namaste/?scope=anon.

ABOUT THE AUTHOR

Sherianna Boyle is the author of eleven books, including her critically acclaimed Emotional Detox book series. She is the founder of Emotional Detox Coaching and the Cleanse Method. Sherianna is a seasoned adjunct psychology, mindfulness, yoga professor and professional speaker. She is certified as a level five Quantum Healer, Master Reiki Teacher, and is host of the *Just Ask Spirit* podcast. When she is not writing, she is probably at the grocery store or hanging out with her husband, KB, and their three daughters. Find her Just Ask Spirit and Emotional Detox retreats, energy healing, Just Ask Spirit School, spirit mentorship, private and group sessions, and classes at sheriannaboyle.com.